Unequivocal Americanism:

Right-Wing Novels in
the Cold War Era

by

MACEL D. EZELL

The Scarecrow Press, Inc.
Metuchen, N. J.   1977

Library of Congress Cataloging in Publication Data

Ezell, Macel D
   Unequivocal Americanism.

   Bibliography: p.
   Includes index.
   1. American fiction--20th century--History and
criticism. 2. Conservatism in literature. I. Title.
PS374.C59E97   813'.03   77-3725
ISBN 0-8108-1033-6

for

Carol

Lynn

Rachel

CONTENTS

ACKNOWLEDGMENTS

For their assistance I am indebted to Harold Currie, Carol Ezell, Jannette Fiore, Donna Gayon, Victor Howard, Douglas Noverr, Russel Nye, Henry Silverman, Edward C. Weber, and the All University Research Committee of Michigan State University.

PREFACE

The idea for this book developed in conjunction with an attempt to look at the development of right-wing groups in the United States in the Cold War era from an interdisciplinary point of view. The number of political, economic, psychological, sociological, and theological studies was almost intimidating. It became apparent, though, that there were few studies which focus upon the literary segments of the conservative movement.

The first question to arise was whether or not there is a body of imaginative literature which could be identified as rightist. It was not difficult to isolate novels published by conservative presses or those offered by patriotic book clubs, nor was it difficult to see patterns of reaction to most books of fiction reviewed in right-wing periodicals; a book is usually clearly acceptable or unacceptable. Right-wing critics evaluate works of fiction by essentially the same criteria that they use to judge the nonfiction works of politicians, economists, ministers, and other writers. In short, it became apparent that novels acceptable to rightists could be identified and analyzed. The potential advantage would be to examine right-wing ideas in a fictional world which is not subjected to historical judgment; such works allow writers to manipulate history to suit their own purposes without having the works rejected for being imaginative.

A second question had to do with scope. For one

vii

whose field of study has been the recent American past, the post-World War II, Cold War era seemed appropriate.

A major obstacle had to do with terminology. One encounters numerous terms which refer to persons or groups that hold political views to the right of center. Conservative, anticommunist, constitutionalist, fundamentalist, free enterpriser, libertarian, individualist, patriot, nationalist, and states' righter are some of the most common. In the United States, three groupings seem appropriate: the moderate majority and the left- and right-wing minorities. Such divisions work well except perhaps for the libertarian elements which have attempted to form a left-right coalition. But few persons are comfortable with the label, right-wing, probably because it has connotations of extremism. The phrase can be understood in a non-pejorative sense, however. In this book it will be used with conservative, rightist, and patriotic to refer to those whose political persuasion can be considered to the right of center--in, it is hoped, a non-condemnatory way.

Although this book deals briefly with background materials, its primary purpose is to provide bibliographical information and isolate some of the major themes in right-wing novels. Besides the fiction itself, I have relied primarily upon book reviews in periodicals which identify themselves as right-wing. Information is also included from a few books of literary criticism endorsed by right-wing spokesmen.

There is no attempt here to determine the volume of sales or the social effects of right-wing literature. Understandably, critical and market appeal of most of the books remain marginal. The major readership undoubtedly consists of "true believers" who want to be confirmed in what they already believe. But the books provide some insights into rightists' thinking.

INTRODUCTION

Novels, poetry, painting, and music are not looked
upon as primary conveyers of rightist thought. Imaginative
literature constitutes only a small part of the mass of right-
wing materials published in the Cold War era. For example,
when in 1969 William H. Chamberlain listed twenty-five significant conservative books of the past quarter century, he
did not list a single novel. [1] This is in keeping with the very
limited number of novelists who publicly identify with right-
wing causes. Of the twenty-nine sponsors of the Conservative
Book Club in 1964, only one, John Dos Passos, was a novelist. [2] Among numerous "named" participants at the fifth
anniversary dinner of National Review, only two were identified as fiction writers: Taylor Caldwell and Dos Passos. [3]
And the national advisory board for Young Americans for
Freedom includes, besides those two, George S. Schuyler,
whose novels were published in the 1930s.

Right-wing spokesmen assign great significance to the
role that imaginative literature can and does play in molding
American attitudes. Hence they enthusiastically greet those
works of art which they think will enhance conservative values.
In the foreword to The Ballad of John Birch (by Douglas
Morse, 1964), E. Merrill Root observes: "We need poetry
today--today we need American poetry. "[4] Rightists insist
that traditional literature has been replaced by the modern
unacceptable varieties. In a Human Events article concerning

1

the Modern Language Association, William A. Hunter quotes
Russell Kirk:

> I believe that English literature has been treated
> with contempt in our schools and our colleges be-
> cause of what a friend of mine calls 'the treason
> of the English teacher. ' ...
>
> The man of letters and the teacher of litera-
> ture have no right to be irresponsible dilettantes or
> reckless iconoclasts; they are placed in their high
> dignity so that they may preserve the ideas which
> make all men one, not so that they may indulge an
> appetite for denigration and a taste for anarchic
> cleverness. [5]

Conservatives are not bashful in asserting that they
are better qualified than liberals to judge what is acceptable
literature.   Ralph de Toledano accused liberal critics of being
unable to "tell Oedipus from apple butter. "[6]   In Triumph,
F. Reid Buckley pointed out why liberals cannot appreciate
or create great works of art.   Being relativists, Buckley explained, liberals are tyrannized by their "dogma of total
permissiveness. "   The liberals' "ideological rejection of
Truth and Order incapacitates" them in recognizing basic virtues. [7]

Content, rather than form, matters to conservatives.
With few exceptions, this survey will deal with content rather
than aesthetics of novels.   Occasionally, rightists discuss the
artistic merits of literature without making plot or message
central.   For example, Robert Beum discussed "The Natural
Law of Poetry" primarily in terms of rhetoric. [8]   But usually style is passed over lightly.   This is not to imply that
conservatives do not care about style, for they are very
sensitive to form, to order.   Yet, in their view, it is not
form as much as meaning that distinguishes good art from
bad.

In essence, right-wing literary criticism has a heavily reactionary, rather than positive, flavor. Rightist publications frequently assert that a liberal bias colors all mainstream publications. They see as part of their task keeping abreast of developments in mainstream media and the pointing out of liberals' errors. And the overwhelming majority of their efforts are spent in objecting to, rather than providing alternatives to, social and intellectual developments. In National Review, a critic writes of living "in a time when most of one's energy goes to discarding, eschewing, rejecting, discovering what one is not."[9]

Right-wing critics look upon their task quite seriously; they consider themselves at war. The lines between them and the enemy are clear-cut, the battle fierce, and the numerical odds in favor of the other side. Although claiming that a single individual, especially one who is committed to traditional values, can overcome scores of the modernists, they still make much of the enemy's ability. And to make matters worse, mass sympathy appears to support the enemy.

Given the odds against winning and the costs of defeat, right-wingers understandably give an apocalyptic tone to their work. A sense of mission permeates right-wing thought--the task, simply put, is to save the republic. Salvation rests upon the small minority that is not only able to see the dangers but is also willing to commit itself to defense of the nation, regardless of cost. In Alpaca two American characters conclude that "when a republic is so threatened, it will be saved--if it is saved--only by people whose political persuasion is to the Right of average."[10] So people of such persuasion make no apologies for their tactics. After all, Medford Evans writes, the conspirators give "contemporary history its apocalyptic quality. It is they who invoke the threat of a Nuclear Doomsday."[11]

Conditions are local and tactics reflect historical developments, but in a sense, the battle reaches far beyond the
present time and place. It fits into an ageless contest.
Again, Medford Evans, a confessed "conspiracy buff,"[12] has
explained the matter: "All history is concerned with con-
spiracies--basically with the Conspiracy."[13] In The Devil's
Advocate, one of Taylor Caldwell's characters notes that "It
was a nightmare and deathly disease with many names. It
was called Fascism and Communism, People's Democracies
and Socialism, the Welfare State and totalitarianism and au-
thoritarianism.... But it was the same foul disease that blinded
and sickened the whole world."[14] With such fuzzy uses of
labels, right-wing writers have no difficulty in lumping together many groups with which they disagree. M. Stanton
Evans can write that the "Kerner report and The Liberal
Papers are, in the final analysis, simply different aspects of
the same befuddled intelligence."[15] Medford Evans can dismiss the "stuffed shirts in The New York Review of Books"
as being the counterparts of the "stuffed T-shirts in Ram-
parts" in that both are "hirelings of the Conspiracy to a man
(or whatever)."[16] The author of The Eagle's Feather can run
together the "tyranny in the labor movement, the perfidy of
the U. S. Supreme Court, and the subversive forces at work
in the mental health movement, education and the nation's
churches."[17]

According to right-wing spokesmen, liberals fail to
see the conspiracy because their attitudes blind them to truth.
Occasionally, of course, a liberal person might appreciate an
Allen Drury novel and even endorse one, but generally a lib-
eral will supposedly accept anti-American art and oppose pro-
American. Lacking transcendent goals and standards, liberals

are subject to being drawn to subversive causes. Being hu-
manistic, they will compromise eternal principles. Lacking
a sense of responsibility for tradition, they tend to equate
"modern" with "good." And being equivocal, they refuse to
condemn, to become indignant. With such proclivities, right-
wingers explain, liberals are understandably defeatists.

Believing that liberals are so vulnerable to criticism,
right-wingers are understandably distraught to find that it is
they, rather than the liberals, who have credibility and popularity problems. They explain the situation by pointing to the
existence of a "Liberal Family." The family is described as
being composed of university professors, Southern bellwethers,
Jews, and other "ADA types." Its purpose is to insure conformity to a left-of-center line in American letters.

The family is able to exercise its power through its
domination of the mass media, according to the rightist
minority. If right-wingers are correct, mainstream (or liberal) reviews boost the works of liberals and damn the efforts of patriotic writers. Right-wingers are convinced that
the population is more conservative than most of the mass
media, but because the masses get only the word of liberals
they do not support the conservatives. Occasionally, though,
a patriotic book receives a positive endorsement, but not
very often. And sometimes a book such as Drury's Advise
and Consent will make the bestseller list and be made into
a popular movie in spite of liberals' reservations. But more
often than not, right-wing spokesmen insist, the "Family"
succeeds in killing right-wing works.

Throughout right-wing circles, The New York Times
is singled out as a special target. According to William A.
Rusher, the newspaper has an "apparent inability to stand for
anything but piecemeal surrender."[18] Occasionally, though,

the Times will publish a favorable review of a book which
right-wingers like.   In such cases, they respond with a statement such as this in regard to Sons of Darkness, Sons of
Light by John A. Williams: " Despite its favorable reviews
in Time and the New York Times Book Review, the book is
worth reading. "[19]   More often though, they are objecting.
Rosalie Gordon of America's Future on several occasions has
accused the paper of "trying to kill" works such as those by
Allen Drury.   She asserted when describing The First Team
by John Ball, that the book belonged at the top of all bestseller lists "but probably got 'the business' because of the
subject: the story of a Soviet take-over of the U. S. and how
it was countered by a small dedicated group of patriots. "[20]
Reviewers in liberal media such as the Times supposedly are
not content to simply pan or ignore right-wing books, but are
accused of going out of their way to launch campaigns to kill
such books. [21]   Thus Forrest Davis could refer to an "open
conspiracy of liberal journalism. "[22]

        In 1967 Rosalie Gordon thought conservatives had
finally won a victory when Senator J. Strom Thurmond (Republican, South Carolina) took up their cause.   The issue
concerned The Spirit of '76 by Holmes Alexander.   According to Thurmond's account in the Congressional Record, the
book, by an author who "must be regarded as an established
author, since he has written 14 books," was "the kind of
book which people like to read. "[23] He buttressed his case
by reading into the record numerous brief newspaper reviews
of the book from across the land--all of which were positive.
But, the Senator explained, he had telephoned 45 bookstores
in the District of Columbia area and had found that only three
stores stocked the book.   None of the bookstores knew the
book well, nor was any enthusiastic about trying to secure
copies.

Thus the Senator suggested that the conservative political ideas of the novel explained its limited availability.
Furthermore, he continued, bookstore proprietors have the
right to follow sound business practices and if a book will
not make a profit, it understandably can be ignored. But,
he hastened to observe, "the proprietor who refuses to carry
a book because he does not want the book unduly read is just
as bad as a bookburner." Even though he admitted that he
had no basis to make charges against individuals, he sus-
pected that there were "bookburners somewhere in the background."[24] The Senator averred that he would give the prob-
lem "increased attention in the future." In response America's Future applauded the Senator's efforts and insisted that
the practice of "bookburning" had been going on for years.[25]
But still the book died a quiet death, unlamented, unnoticed
by mainstream reviewers.

Not all right-wing critics see the matter in simple,
conspiratorial terms. For example, Guy Davenport, a frequent critic in National Review, has referred to "a liberal
attitude that may be native to the arts in general."[26] But
reviews of novels in such periodicals as National Review,
American Opinion, America's Future, and Human Events reflect that Davenport's explanation is not nearly as prominent
as other conspiratorial theories.

There is a wide range of sophistication among right-
wing statements about fiction. Even in the same publication,
some reviewers appear as unabashedly doctrinaire while others are coolly professional. For example, a reading of reviews by Revilo Oliver or E. Merrill Root and Hugh Kenner,
Robert Phelps, or Davenport will make clear very different
tones. The first two are admitted partisans; the other three
are noticeably more objective and professional.

Although there are right-wing organizations which significantly differ from one another, there are obvious over-
lappings of membership and writers. It is not unusual to find
a writer appearing in publications in several periodicals.
When Human Events celebrated its twenty-fifth anniversary,
it contained greetings from organizations and officers of such
groups from across a broad spectrum of right-wing opinion.
And the Conservative Book Club (a part of the National Review sector of the right-wing) advertises in periodicals in
several categories of organizations. Hence a novel acceptable
to one periodical will likely be well received in others also.

NOTES

1. Human Events, 12 April 1969, pp. 49-51.

2. Advertisement, National Review, 16 June 1964, p. 505.

3. National Review, 22 October 1960, p. 228.

4. E. Merrill Root, Foreword to The Ballad of John Birch,
    by Douglas Morse (Brookfield, Mass.: The County
    Press, 1964), p. 10.

5. William A. Hunter, "Modern Language Ass'n: An
    Example of our Academic Problems," Human Events,
    21 June 1975, p. 512.

6. Ralph de Toledano, "When the Big Job Is at Stake," re-
    view of The Big Man, by Henry J. Taylor, in Na-
    tional Review, 4 May 1964, p. 360.

7. F. Reid Buckley, "Liberalism and Literature," Triumph,
    February 1968, pp. 26-29.

8. Robert Beum, "The Natural Law of Poetry," ibid., No-
    vember 1968, pp. 34-37.

9. Review of Logarithms, by James L. Weil, in National
    Review, 26 October 1957, p. 382.

10. H. L. Hunt, Alpaca Revisited (Dallas: HLH Products, 1967), p. 41.

11. Medford Evans, Review of Captains and Kings, by Taylor Caldwell in American Opinion, June 1972, p. 85.

12. Medford Evans, Review of The Rosa Luxemburg Contraceptive Cooperative, by Leopold Tyrmand, in American Opinion, December 1972, p. 87.

13. Medford Evans, Review of Captains and Kings, p. 77.

14. Taylor Caldwell, The Devil's Advocate (New York: Macfadden-Bartell Corporation, 1964), p. 333.

15. M. Stanton Evans, "The Violent Explain It Away," Review of Preserve and Protect, by Allen Drury, in National Review, 3 December 1968, p. 1225.

16. Medford Evans, Review of Captains and Kings, p. 83.

17. William Campbell Douglass, The Eagle's Feather (New Orleans: Free Men Speak, Inc., 1966), pp. 125-126.

18. William A. Rusher, "Modern Morality Play," Review of A Shade of Difference, by Allen Drury, in National Review, 6 November 1962, p. 357.

19. G. K. Potter, Review of Sons of Darkness, Sons of Light, by John A. Williams, in Triumph, January 1970, p. 35.

20. Rosalie Gordon, "More Terrific 'Fiction,'" Review of The First Team, by John Ball, in America's Future, 10 November 1972, p. 6.

21. Gordon, "The 'Times' and 'The Fountainhead,'" America's Future, 18 October 1968, pp. 5-7.

22. Forrest Davis, "The Age of the Shrug," Review of Advise and Consent, by Allen Drury, National Review, 29 August 1959, p. 306.

23. U.S., Congress, Senate, Senator J. Strom Thurmond, "Suppression of Books," 90th Cong., 1st Sess., 21 February 1967, Congressional Record, 133:4120.

24. <u>Ibid.</u> , p. 4121.

25. "More Book Burners," <u>America's Future</u>, 7 April 1967, pp. 5-6.

26. Guy Davenport, "Apocalypse Next Exit," <u>National Review</u>, 1 December 1970, p. 1303.

CHAPTER I

BACKGROUND

Right-wing organizations in the United States since
World War II have been highly visible. While reactionary
movements undoubtedly hold only minority status, their per-
vasiveness and shrillness reflect the general tensions of the
society--widespread tensions which have resulted from rapid,
drastic social change. Hence consideration of right-wing literature logically begins with a survey of some of the general conditions of the times and responses to them. The
twentieth century has been an era when rapid social changes
have led to challenges to traditional institutions and values.
The resulting insecurity is undoubtedly the basis for extremist groups.

One need not be a Marxist to see the significance of
economic issues in twentieth century American life. The extreme fluctuations between prosperity and depression, the
ugly environmental problems associated with the American
industrial revolution, and obvious increases in the gap between the affluent and the poor, as well as other economic
problems, raised questions which went to the heart of the
American way of life. Dramatically and traumatically the
Great Depression forced Americans to consider alternatives
to the existing system. Although far from being a complete
restructuring of the old order, the New Deal renovated certain parts of the structure. The preliminary steps toward a

welfare state--Social Security and the Tennessee Valley Authority, for example--were new developments in the American system.

As the nation moved toward a welfare state, the role of the federal government necessarily changed. The addition of new social duties combined with the assumption of wartime obligations resulted in a very noticeable increase in the size of the bureaucracies and the budgets. No longer serving merely as a policeman whose major job was to protect private property, the central government was to provide leadership, to plan economic growth. In addition, it was charged with protecting the underdogs, the victims of exploitation.

Not only did the role of the federal government change in domestic matters, it changed also in international affairs. Wittingly or no, in entering World War II and emerging a victor it found itself with a world leadership role. It had muffed its chances of becoming a major voice in the League of Nations; from some angles it was accused of being responsible for the failure of the League and for the coming of the war. And the accounts of atrocities in Europe, where an estimated six to nine million people died in the wake of totalitarian movements, made the accusation more biting. Americans, then, were committed to playing a different role in the world, a role which would require a strong central government.

But they were not prepared to accept readily the frustrations which seem to be concomitant parts of world leadership. The issues in World War II had been defined in simple terms. It had been described as a struggle between freedom and tyranny. When the Allies won, according to wartime propaganda, the world should have been a happy place in which to live. Such was not to be the case.

The war resulted in a change in the world balance of

power.   The western European democracies were relegated
to second-rate powers which looked to the United States for
leadership.   Moscow emerged from the war as the center of
a coalition of nations committed to communism--which soon
came to be looked upon as negatively as fascism had been.
With the establishment of a Marxist state in China and the
Russian explosion of an atomic device, world tensions evoked
apocalyptic interpretations.   There would likely have to be
another showdown between the east and west.   This time,
though, atomic weapons could destroy all life on the planet.
Unfortunately, the United Nations, which was supposed to be
effectively different from previous endeavors at international
cooperation, could do little to lessen international tensions.

In view of the fears concerning the domestic economy,
the exigencies of war, and the tensions of the Cold War, the
political parties in the United States tended to move toward
a common platform.   Consensus politics came to be the basic
approach, whether in political campaigns, congressional legis-
lation, or executive action.   Domestic problems played second place to foreign; hence the need for a unified stand in
world affairs meant that major differences over internal matters were not always openly and clearly debated.

While the economic and political changes were taking
place, secondary effects were becoming apparent.   The rapid
urbanization which continued after World War II would have
reverberations across American society.   As people left the
farms and moved to the city, the urban areas found that the
number of problems increased with the population.   And it
was the ugly, unfortunate developments--crime, squalor, pol-
lution--which attracted the most attention.   The ex-rural
residents were ill-equipped to deal with city problems, so
the problems tended to increase as the affluent residents began

an exodus to the suburbs, leaving the central areas of cities
to decay even faster.

At the time when political and economic changes were
creating sharp tensions, they were also weakening traditional
institutions such as the church and the family, institutions
which formerly had provided stability and guidance in times
of crises. As the nation became more prosperous and urban,
it became less spiritual--at least by traditional norms. Law-
lessness, violence, and displacement were far more visible
than they had been before. The divorce rate increased year
by year.

As the nation became more urban and secular, its
people became more cosmopolitan. Serving in the armed
forces, living in metropolitan areas, and reaching higher educational levels, the generations of the 1950s and 1960s reflected characteristics not previously identified with Americanism. Young people, whose ranks would be exploded by
the war-baby boom, who had not known the Great Depression
and World War II, adopted life styles which seemed to flaunt
traditional ways. In dress, in music, and in other ways,
their tastes differed drastically from their parents'.

Eventually the youths became involved in protest poli-
tics--to some extent an outgrowth of the civil rights movement. Near the turn of the century, W. E. B. DuBois
pointed out that the color line would be the crucial issue in
the new century. After World War II his comment was un-
deniably confirmed. Restive black GIs returned from the
war unwilling to accept the subservient positions previously
allotted them. Sensing this animosity and being aware of
racial conflicts which had followed World War I, the Truman
administration made at least token efforts to allay racial con-
frontations. Then came Brown vs. Board of Education, Mar-

tin Luther King, Jr., Malcolm X, and other forces which,
by mobilizing black people, created uneasy feelings among
the majority.   Riots in Detroit, Watts, Newark and other
cities further heightened anxieties.

The armed intervention in Viet Nam served as a uni-
fying point for the disenchanted, restless minorities.   Youths,
blacks, and others were united informally by the opposition
they shared.   And a "counterculture," ill-defined though it
may have been, seemed to reflect a new order which cut
across all segments of national life and which involved far
more than opposition to the war.

To a significant extent, all of the changes and up-
heavals which followed World War II were accentuated, if not
produced by, American mass media.   By supplementing and
visualizing the coverage of newspapers and magazines, television became the major source of information in American
homes.   As protest movements spread and gained intensity,
the media seemed to be focused upon them.   Daily, Americans witnessed, via live or filmed television coverage, protests across the land.

All the changes and tensions led to a questioning, if
not alteration, of traditional American values and institutions.
In general, the American "dream" seemed to have become a
nightmare.   The ability of democracy to deal with social
problems came to be questioned.   So did the equity of a competitive economic system.   Likewise, traditional religions
faced severe tests.   But while most Americans likely sensed
a feeling of insecurity, they did not lose faith in the system.
They accepted social change as a necessity and relied upon
traditional institutions to adapt to a new world.   Consensus
politics, compromise diplomacy, and moderate welfarism
created no moral crisis for them.   They tried to cope with

an urban, secular culture without undue anxiety.

There were others, though--people who saw only defeat and failure in the direction the nation was taking, groups
which maintained that only by restoring the best of a golden
past could the nation survive. They spoke in apocalyptic
tones about the sinister trends they saw. So far, no simple
definition has been devised that would cover all the groups
or issues which have been labeled "right-wing." Even so, it
is possible to describe some of the characteristics of such
groups and see some of the ties which bind them together in
a general, though amorphous, camp.

Not all advocates of extremely conservative notions
withdrew from mainstream circles. In politics, for example,
both Democratic and Republican parties continued to have
powerful, verbal segments which sought to align the parties
with a right-wing platform. In 1948 the Democrats saw the
Dixiecrats withdraw and run J. Strom Thurmond in opposition
to Truman. And George C. Wallace of Alabama, sometimes
labeled more populist than reactionary, but never liberal,
has posed a severe challenge in recent years. But the Republicans have been the more likely of the two to represent
a conservative alternative to New Deal Democrats. The surprising defeat of Thomas Dewey in 1948, the victory of
Dwight Eisenhower over Robert Taft for the Republican nomination in 1952, the failure of the Eisenhower administration
to undo the welfare state, and the overwhelming trouncing of
Barry Goldwater by Lyndon Johnson in 1964 made the party
an unpromising channel through which right-wingers might
secure their political goals, but they still remained, finding
some consolation in the senatorial victories of Goldwater,
John Tower, and other arch conservatives.

But to supplement the work of existing institutions,

right-wing advocates have established and supported thousands
of organizations since World War II.   The nature, size and
longevity of the groups have been so tenuous that no one has
been able to compile a satisfactory listing.   Hence the precise numbers and specific goals of the organizations have
never been cataloged.   Their influence is even more unclear.
It is possible, nevertheless, to delineate several categories
into which most of the groups can be placed.   There are
overlaps, of course, but these categories are convenient ways
of getting at the mass of right-wing groups.

 Anticommunist groups.   Anticommunism is undoubtedly
the most common surface issue among right-wing groups.
The unorganized following of Senator Joseph McCarthy in the
1950s was one such group; though not formally an organization, it generated an enormous publicity campaign and undoubtedly influenced national policies, both domestic and
diplomatic.   Another group, much more formal in structure
but less significant in its influence, is the John Birch Society.
Its Western Islands Press has published numerous nonfiction
books and a limited number of novels.   Many other right-
wing groups identify themselves as primarily anticommunist
in purpose.

 Religion.   Other right-wing groups have taken religion
as the basis of their identification.   These include F. Schwarz'
Christian Anticommunism Crusade, Billy James Hargis' Christian Crusade, Carl McIntyre's Twentieth Century Reformation
Hour, and the Church League of America, which is not as
closely identified with a single name as the others.   Among
Catholics, publishers of Triumph support right-wing causes,
and the American Jewish League against Communism has
been supported by persons such as Roy M. Cohn, one of
Joseph McCarthy's investigators.

Racism. Although they seldom publicly claim anti-
black prejudice as the basis for their groups, organizations
such as White Citizens Councils, the Ku Klux Klan, and
Kent and Phoebe Courtney's Conservative Society of America
obviously exist primarily as advocates of white racial interests. And Common Sense, which ceased publication in 1972,
was characterized by a strong antisemitism.

Capitalism. Economic groups often use patriotism or
anticommunism as surface issues when they are in fact committed primarily to the laissez-faire capitalism of the nineteenth-century United States. Examples of such groups would
include H. L. Hunt's Lifeline, Christian Economics, and The
Freeman.

Education. Some right-wing groups operate under the
guise of educational institutions. The National Education
Program, a satellite of Harding College, Searcy, Arkansas,
is one such endeavor, and the Douglas MacArthur School of
Americanism at Howard Payne College, Brownwood, Texas
is another. Bob Jones University, established to champion
fundamentalist evangelical Protestantism, is also noted for
its identification with right-wing causes.

Libertarianism. Libertarians form another segment
of the right-wing. Although the label applies to a very dis-
parate grouping of individualists, the Ayn Rand Objectivists
form the group which has the highest profile in this category.
An unabashed elitism often characterizes persons who represent these groups. And though a few persons might claim
to favor "libertarian socialism" or some other quasi-coopera-
tive scheme, groups in this area are usually advocates of a
competitive order.

Scholars have approached the study of right-wing
groups from a number of perspectives. So far, though, none

has been able to bring the various approaches (historical, sociological, political, psychological) together in a unified, final way. A major problem stems from an inability to delineate just what sets an extremist apart from a person who is not. As a matter of fact, there has been no convincing definition of what a "normal" or "moderate" person or group is. In many ways, people tagged as extremists function in the ordinary world in ordinary ways. Even though the divisions of left and right apply only in a very nebulous way as categories for people, such groupings do serve to analyze certain mind sets and political ideologies. Since certain individuals and groups claim the label, even glory in it, the use of "right-wing," "rightist," and other such designations has become a part of the American vocabulary. One way to understand the movement is to consider personality factors which tend to make people susceptible to right-wing causes.

The most noticeable characteristics of right-wingers often involve insecurity and alienation. Insecure, alienated people seem to find in right-wing (or left-wing, for that matter) causes some outlet which eases if not eliminates the sources of their discontent. Sociologists have focused upon status anxieties as a major cause of right-wingers' insecurities. In a rapidly changing society some individuals and groups move upward on the socio-economic ladder. Others find themselves blocked from upward movement, being left behind, or losing ground to other groups. The measure of status varies but the common problem seems to be the sense of threats to or loss of "place"--measured either by the real exercise of power or by symbolic impotence. Groups which have been identified include small, independent businessmen and other economic groups who operate on the fringe of the American economy, persons in certain professions (such as

medicine and the ministry) which formerly held a relatively
higher symbolic place in the community than they now do.

Another apparent cause of right-wing insecurity has to
do with education, or the lack of it. Although some out-
croppings of right-wing extremism may be composed of relatively highly educated people (Senator Goldwater's supporters
in 1964, for example), the groups generally are composed of
people with modest educational attainments. Such persons
often find themselves poorly prepared to do well in a highly
technical, mobile society. Understandably they are likely
not to favor complex, neutral explanations over simplistic,
doctrinaire ones. They also prefer heroic, committed leaders to moderate bureaucrats who do not divide issues into
"good" and "bad" categories. Ambiguity is anathema, sim-
plicity is virtuous. Hence, scholars have pointed out that
right-wingers tend to be close-minded rather than open-
minded. They need "hard, cold facts." Once they have
them, they feel no need to look further. They only want
substantiation of what they know.

Being defensive people who feel that somehow mainstream life has passed them by, right-wingers react very
strongly against "being pushed around." Generally, secure
people can accept restrictions (in the name of community
welfare or efficiency) more easily than can minority people
who consider themselves outsiders. Right-wingers, of course,
do not explain their over-reaction by pointing to their insecurity; they are more likely to identify with the libertarian tradition which has long been a part of American mythology.

In common with other minority or extremist groups,
right-wingers also tend to be more paranoiac than non-extrem-
ists. To them, the central facts of life revolve around
their social-political-economic commitments. Having taken

unambiguous stands, they expect persecution.   Events which
to other people would be no cause for great concern or specu-
lation reflect serious implications if one expects and looks
for conspiracies.   According to right-wingers, only brain-
washed or naive persons fail to see the threats.

Right-wingers tend to be dogmatic about a set of ab-
solutes--the particulars may vary from group to group or
from person to person.   The horror they oppose is the wil-
lingness of liberals or moderates to compromise.   In keeping
with a tendency to simplify life along two lines--right and
wrong, correct and incorrect, acceptable and unacceptable--
rightists are quick to draw lines and identify enemies.

Claiming clear understanding of, and offering concrete
definitions of both worthy and sinister forces, right-wingers
take the next step of demanding loyalty to the "good" and opposition to the "evil."   Criticisms of anomalies of national
life can be disregarded in view of the relative merits of the
system, especially when such failures are contrasted to the
demerits of alternatives.   Understandably, rightists have little regard for dissidents who loudly call attention to ugly aspects of the culture.

Even if dissidents have complaints, the criticisms,
according to rightists, should be offered in a nonthreatening
way.   Rightists are often noticeably more threatened by agi-
tators than are moderates; stated differently, they value stability and security more than reform.   Mobs of noisy com-
plainers--whether the protesters be opposing government
policies concerning civil rights, poverty, or diplomacy--
threaten the system.   Only rarely do right-wingers resort to
mass protests.   Even then their assemblies tend to be in
honor of some specific patriot or in support of some pro-
posal rather than take the form of mass disobedience.   In

recent years, though, the school busing controversy has
drawn some rightists into mass action.

They base their opposition to change upon a respect
for old ways. Several anthropologists have described tribal
instincts to build up myths about the origins and early greatness of societies. When questions of change arise, therefore, there is a strong urge on the part of loyalists to maintain as close ties as possible to the ways of early days.
Often the conception of the past to which there is an identification may be distorted if not completely mythologized, but
the reverence it generates plays a strong role in determining
the values of conservatives. Obviously, American right-
wingers are not the only ones who are influenced by such
values, for the cry of "they have forsaken the ways of their
elders" has been a part of man's cry from biblical times,
if not earlier.

There is an apparent tie between an extreme reverence for the past and a strong sense of nationalism. And
again, the United States is not unique in having verbal, highly visible patriots. Not unlike "love," nationalism is an ab-
straction which seems to defy precise definition. Yet no one
can deny its prominent emphasis in right-wing literature.
Especially is it apparent in the postwar years when there has
been a renewed effort to improve international cooperation.
Almost without exception, opposition to the United Nations
has been a major tenet of right-wing groups. They also
have tended to oppose friendly commercial, scientific or cul-
tural exchange programs with nonwestern nations.

At times, certain elements of the right-wing appear
to be isolationist. But a fervent anticommunism as the
counterpart of a strong nationalism has tempted right-wing
groups to urge the federal government to take up the cause

of opposing, if not stamping out altogether, communist movements around the world.   And while some of them have supported mutual defense organizations such as NATO and
SEATO, rightists generally urge that the United States play
the role of unilateral leader, with invitations to others to
join on American terms.   The basis for this argument has
been that with super-weapons and superior delivery capability,
the nation has not needed other countries and that to involve
them in policy-making would mean only that the United States
would unnecessarily sacrifice its interests since it has nothing, or very little, to gain from allowing others to participate in decision-making.

        To some extent, other values identified with right-
wing groups have tended to qualify the overarching national-
istic trappings.   Opposition to the federal government is one
example.   Although the right-wing cause in the South may
have more to do with race issues than with others, the apparent regional tones in right-wing propaganda in the South-
west and far West would indicate that agreement on national
values is far from unified.   Another regional tie has to do
with religion.   There has been a temptation to identify right-
wing causes with religious fundamentalism in the Bible Belt.
There are obvious parallels between the simplistic, dogmatic
religious sympathies of the evangelical groups and right-wing
patriotic groups, but there are qualifications which must
temper this line of thinking, for there have been apparent
sympathies between conservative Catholics and right-wing
groups also.   Ultimately a set of questions concerns whether
right-wing religious groups spawn and support patriotic groups
or whether both stem from a more basic set of circumstances.

        Agrarianism has possibly been more directly influen-
tial than religion or region on right-wing thinking.   The basic

institutions of the nation were conceived as the best ones for people in rural, agrarian pursuits. Correctly or incorrectly, both American government and American Christianity have been identified closely with an idealized independent yeoman farmer who, according to the myth, established the nation primarily to purge both government and religion of corrupting influences. In the pristine New World, the individual man supposedly could be his own master. Given independence and an opportunity to work directly in touch with nature, early Americans, the myth goes, experienced a golden age--an age which declined with the coming of the American industrial revolution with its consequent ugliness and complexities. Right-wingers believe that it is still possible to maintain local control and individual freedom, and that a return to conditions of the golden age is possible. In essence, the values advocated closely follow the idealized agrarian ones advocated by a great number of American spokesmen from Crèvecoeur through Jefferson to the flower children of the 1960s.

But the agrarian mentality does not explain the interests of hyper-patriotic Americans in world affairs. Instead, one looks to the manifest destiny notions that were formulated in nineteenth-century American thought. The United States is not merely to maintain physical superiority but, to right-wingers, barring only those of isolationist sympathies, the nation should support "freedom" around the world. Particularly incumbent upon the nation is a moral--if not religious--obligation to oppose and defeat the machinations of communists. Whereas in nineteenth-century thinking there was a positive emphasis upon spreading democracy and Christianity, in recent years a more noticeable emphasis has been placed upon negative anticommunism.

Another negative value of the right concerns the atti-

tudes of its partisans toward educated specialists, especially
those whose training has to do with social theories: economists, political scientists, historians, sociologists, psychologists, and others. Even though spokesmen for rightist
causes employ degrees, scholarly techniques such as foot-
notes, bibliographies and the like, as well as other apparent
counterparts of the liberal world's authority symbols, there
is a consistent anti-intellectual emphasis which runs throughout right-wing literature. Furthermore, this is only one
element of populism which the right-wing has taken up. Others include anti-eastern, anti-aristocratic themes, and sometimes antisemitic ones as well, although most right-wing organizations are careful to avoid activities and statements
which might make them appear to be blatantly antisemitic.

    Almost without exception right-wingers have reacted
negatively to civil rights movements. Hence they have often
been identified with the racist doctrines of white supremacy.
Few people, of course, admit to being racist, and rightists
are no exception. Usually they speak in terms of local control, of freedom of choice, or of the rights of property own-
ers. So far, relatively few studies have focused precisely
upon what role racist ideas have played in right-wing thinking, to what extent euphemisms such as "states' rights" are
really attempts to deal with racial questions indirectly. It
is apparent, though, that the racial history of the United
States has given it a unique set of problems, and it is also
likely that a major difference between European and American rightist movements has to do with the presence of Afro-
Americans in the society, in the past as slaves, in the present as free persons.

    In some cases, right-wingers see themselves set
apart from the masses by a superiority not necessarily re-

lated to race.   Believing themselves to be fortunate, successful persons, they claim to have earned their privileges.   But
economic success is not the only measure they use.   They
often assume an H. L. Mencken pose of intellectual and cul-
tural elitism.   And nearly always there is an implied, if
not literal, claim to moral purity.

The mass media generally have treated the right-wing
as ugly malcontents if not outright crackpots.   And as right-
wing spokesmen themselves have at times admitted, they tend
to have a very limited and poorly used sense of humor.
Consequently they have frequently come across as sour-faced
preachers of doom who speak down to the masses from their
self-proclaimed pinnacles of virtue.

Not only do right-wingers create an image of hard-
nosed Puritans, they advocate such aggressive solutions to
problems, domestic and foreign, that they often appear to be
militaristic if not fascistic.   At times they condone restrict-
ing certain freedoms in the name of defending others.   In
foreign affairs, particularly, they tend to see overkill as an
effective means of solving problems.   They react in horror
to the notion that compromise and negotiation are preferable
to and at times more effective than the use of force.   And
nowhere does the temperament of the rightist appear more
dramatically than in reaction to dissident citizens.   Deporta-
tion, internment, and other extreme penalties are advocated
for those citizens who will not profess their uncompromising
commitment to the country.   Unusual dress, language, and
other behaviorial symbols also evoke angry reactions.   In
short, right-wingers appreciate a neat, orderly citizenry
which works carefully within the system.   Only such people,
patriots believe, deserve freedom.

CHAPTER II

ACCEPTABLE WRITERS AND NOVELS

There are few book-length statements of rightists' literary standards. Several general books which tend to be more social than literary in emphasis, such as those by Jeffrey Hart and Russell Kirk, provide philosophical statements but deal only indirectly with novels and poetry. Two books have received endorsement by right-wing reviewers: John Beaty's Image of Life, now somewhat out of date since it was published in 1940, and Trousered Apes: A Study in the Influence of Literature on Contemporary Society, by Duncan Williams, first published in England in 1971 and later published in the United States by a conservative publishing house and made available through the Conservative Book Club.

But such books provide only limited statements. To get at what rightists expect of imaginative literature, this study first briefly identifies some of the writers and summarizes some novels which have been well received by right-wing spokesmen. Then it takes note of some of the writers and novels to which right-wingers have objected. Finally, it treats basic themes which rightists would have novelists emphasize.

So far no rightist group has taken belle lettres as its primary concern. But a number of periodicals have included reviews of novels, poetry, and other art forms. The following survey provides an overview of some of the writers whose

27

works have been well received in right-wing circles.   Among
the major ones are Allen Drury, John Dos Passos, Taylor
Caldwell, and Ayn Rand.

Among American writers whose works have been acceptable to right-wing critics, one of the most successful in
the market place is Allen Drury.   A Texan by birth, Drury
grew up in California.   After being discharged from military
service for medical reasons in 1943, he went to Washington,
D. C. , where he became a reporter for United Press.   After
fifteen years' reporting on the Senate, the last ones on the
staff of the New York Times, Drury published his first novel
in 1959.   Its success made it possible for him to become a
roving reporter for Reader's Digest.   Over the next fifteen
years he wrote seven long novels and some nonfiction books
as well.   For Advise and Consent he received the Pulitzer
Prize in 1960, and most of his novels have made the bestseller lists.
        Six of Drury's novels concern the same basic char-
acters and deal with the same themes.   Advise and Consent
(1959), the best received of Drury's novels, focuses upon
the workings of the United States Senate.   The unnamed
President nominates Robert Leffingwell to be Secretary of
State, a nomination which is controversial because of accu-
sations that the nominee associated with a disloyal group
years before and because of his generally liberal views.
Senator Brigham Anderson is appointed chairman of a sub-
committee of the Senate Foreign Relations Committee to hear
witnesses and make a report on Leffingwell.   Senator Seab
Cooley of South Carolina uses the occasion to try to block
Leffingwell's appointment.   As the President and other party
leaders begin to apply pressure to insure confirmation of the

candidate, Senator Anderson learns that Leffingwell has not
been truthful.   The Senator also finds himself the subject of
blackmail attempts.   The President, a Supreme Court Justice,
the Senate majority leader, and a militant liberal Senator,
Fred Van Ackerman of Wyoming, eventually learn of, and allow
to be exposed an account of Anderson's homosexual experience
during his military service.   His suicide follows and the President's nominee is defeated.   The President dies, leaving Harley Hudson, the new President, to name his own Secretary of
State.   Meanwhile, the Russians have landed on and laid claim
to the moon and have demanded that the United States send
representatives to Geneva to discuss implications of their
achievement.

    The heroes of the book are conservative senators such
as Cooley of South Carolina, and Orrin Knox, a Robert Taft-
like man from Illinois, who put integrity above politics and
who prefer firmness to equivocation.   They want an end to
what they describe as "this flabby damned mushy nothingness"
that lies behind the dry rot which has allowed the nation to
fall from its pre-eminence.

    A Shade of Difference (1962) takes up the presidency
of Harley Hudson and deals primarily with the mistreatment
of the United States by the Afro-Asian representatives in the
United Nations.   The plot focuses upon the trip to the United
States by His Royal Highness Terrence Wolowo Ajkaje, the
M'Bulu of Mbuele (also known as "Terrible Terry"), ruler of
Grotoland.   He comes to New York to pressure the United
Nations to demand that Great Britain grant independence to
his land immediately, rather than in a year as announced.
Under tutelage of leftists, the young man makes a side trip
to South Carolina and participates in a mass anti-segregation
rally.   He is roughed-up by whites and uses the treatment

as a basis to seek United Nations condemnation of the United
States for its racial policies.   The resolution is defeated by
the use of the veto by the United States.   The Soviet Union,
mover behind the show, suddenly decides to support the
M'Bulu's cousin who has initiated an uprising against the ab-
sent prince.   In spite of his unwelcomed actions, the United
States sides with the established ruler who has been embarrassing the United States.

The story ends with President Hudson beset by com-
munist-supported uprisings abroad and lack of support at
home.

Most black people in the story come across quite
negatively.   Only one, Cullee Hamilton, a representative
from California, emerges as an attractive person.   He refuses to be anything but a loyal American and decent person,
even though it means losing his wife, who forsakes him for
the likes of "Terrible Terry" and LeGage Shelby, leader of
DEFY (Defenders of Equality for You), a militant civil rights
group.   The protagonists of the novel are the ones who oppose "giving in" to the U.S.S.R. in its quest for world conquest.

Capable of Honor (1965) takes up where A Shade of
Difference leaves off.   When rebels in Grotoland kill some
American missionaries and destroy some of an American oil
company's property, President Hudson sends in American
troops.   He also sends troops into Panama, where another
rebellion has started.   The nation is almost equally divided
between those who support and oppose the military involve-
ments.   The major villain is a pompous, liberal newspaper
columnist, Walter Dobius, whose word is so persuasive that
almost without exception the "liberal Establishment" follows
his lead.   Governor Edward (Ted) Jason of California, a

liberal, and Senator Orrin Knox of Illinois, a conservative, would both like to become president. But President Hudson, son of a Grand Rapids, Michigan, furniture dealer, chooses to try to go for a four-year term to secure approval of his foreign policies. He tells Jason and Knox that the vice presidency is open for the one who can win it.

The national party convention, which is the primary event of the book, is a nasty affair. Inspired by radical groups but blamed on Knox forces, riots break out. As the result of a savage beating by protesters, Knox's pregnant daughter-in-law miscarries. President Hudson appears to have lost adequate support to win the nomination, so Jason challenges him for the presidential nomination on the convention floor. But the Senator loses. Then Hudson demands Knox as his vice presidential running mate. Jason, supported by COMFORT (Committee on Making Further Offers for a Russian Truce), KEEP (Konference on Efforts to Encourage Patriotism), and DEFY, walks out, apparently to run as an independent.

In this novel, the protagonists are men and women who value and personify truth, honor, integrity and, above all, patriotism. Robert Leffingwell, who was defeated by Knox forces in Advise and Consent, repudiates his former friends and nominates Hudson for the presidency. The liberals and their camp followers are disloyal, brutal, unprincipled persons who find that Jason's equivocation makes him an acceptable candidate. The major theme, though, concerns the unfair, unpatriotic, poisonous bias of the news media.

Hudson's victory is short-lived--as Preserve and Protect continues the story. When his plane lands in Washington on its return from California where the convention has met, its landing mechanism does not function properly, and

the President dies in a fiery crash.   The Russians, of course,
are responsible, but just how is not clear.   Hudson's death
leaves open the presidential nomination.   Again there is a battle between Jason and Knox, with Jason's Russian-manipulated
friends resorting to legal maneuvering and unethical shenanigans to keep Knox from receiving the nomination.   But he
does, and Jason promises to repudiate violence if he is put
on the ticket as vice presidential nominee.   Through four
hundred pages the reader follows the political thinking of the
cast of characters.

     For the conclusion of the Advise and Consent series,
Drury has written two books.   In Come Nineveh, Come Tyre
(1973), Orrin Knox is killed and Edward Jason becomes president.   Immediately he orders withdrawal of American troops
from Grotoland and Panama.   He is ordered to meet Russian
officials who demand that he agree to terms that will make
the United States a weakened vassal state in the Soviet Empire.   Too late President Jason learns what has been apparent to the reader from the beginning of Advise and Consent,
that the U.S.S.R. is out to destroy the United States.   Real-
izing his error, he commits suicide, leaving the nation defeated and in subservience to Russia.

     In Promise of Joy (1975) Drury has Jason killed and
Knox become president.   Knox refuses to bow to Russian demands that the United States get out of Grotoland and Panama.
It appears that finally the two nuclear superpowers will have
a military showdown.   But not so.   Rather, the U.S.S.R.
and China get into a nuclear shootout.   Former opponents of
the United States in the United Nations and even Russian leaders humbly beg President Knox to intervene, but he refuses
until the two giants have nearly annihilated one another.   Then
he steps in--on which side is unclear.   So all ends well for

the United States, thanks to the election of a Robert Taft-like conservative as president.

In Throne of Saturn (1970) the same basic themes prevail even though the book does not fit into the Advise and Consent series. In response to liberal columnists, union leaders, and other "anti-Americans," the President forces a Jew and a black into a space crew. The President also disallows the arming of the space ship. When the craft finally gets to the moon on the first leg of a much longer space trip, an armed Russian force almost destroys the American project. The Jewish astronaut, who turns out to be romantically attached to the commander of the vehicle, dies as a result of a wound received in a conflict with Russians on the moon. The commander has to shoot the black astronaut because he attempts to ditch his American craft and crew to join forces with the Russians, who really do not want him. Heroically, the commander returns the craft and saves the black astronaut's life. The story ends with the President's dramatic repudiation of further political interference in the space program and his firm commitment that future space craft will be armed.

After Advise and Consent, Drury's books have been received positively only by critics in conservative and popular media. Mass market book purchasers have treated his work generously. Liberal critics have dismissed them as doctrinaire tracts which lack artistic merit. And at times reviewers in conservative journals have apparently been hard pressed to write positively of his work, for they sometimes begin with the lame statement that the book under consideration is better than the liberals claim. One reviewer in National Review has suggested that Drury's works be viewed as morality plays.[1] Another suggested that they should be viewed as history. M. Stanton Evans wrote that Drury describes the way things are more clearly than do Arthur Schlesinger, Jr. or Theodore Sorensen. [2] Forrest Davis believed that Advise and Consent "may be the first authentically great American political novel. "[3] He also noted:

> It is as if an accumulated distaste for the cliche-ridden, deracinated, anti-traditional and other-directed establishment ruling our political discourse and cheerfully digging the Republic's grave, had forced the author into sophisticated disclosure. [4]

No one has been more enthusiastic about Drury than Rosalie Gordon, editor of America's Future. Ferdinand V. Solara has described her writing as having a "calm, convincing tone" and "thorough documentation. "[5] In Gordon's review of Come Nineveh, Come Tyre, entitled "Great, Great, Great!" she described the book as "the most important political document of our time. "[6]

Drury has not identified himself with right-wing causes as openly as some other writers have done. In contrast to John Dos Passos and Taylor Caldwell, he has not publicly supported such causes as the Conservative Book Club, nor has he written for or been interviewed in such periodicals as National Review and American Opinion. His most extensive statement about his political views appeared in Ayn Rand's Objectivist in 1969. [7]

John Dos Passos (1896-1970) has undoubtedly earned more respect for his artistic achievements than any other writer claimed by right-wingers. After World War II, he wrote as negatively of the New Deal, labor unions, and communism as he had of the established institutions of earlier years. Party line-oriented reviewers, of course, especially

those who earlier had complimented the author, accused him
of selling out or of never having been a convert. Non-doc-
trinaire critics were more concerned about Dos Passos' loss
of creative energy than about his change of thinking on social
issues. Right-wing critics enthusiastically welcomed Dos
Passos into their circles. Seldom building specific, positive
cases for the artistic merits of his later works, they accused
his detractors of being nonthinking, line-hewing hacks, if not
outright subversives. In becoming a sponsor of the Conservative Book Club, a contributor to publications such as National
Review, and a publicized friend of conservatives such as
William F. Buckley, Jr., Dos Passos was apparently happy
to be identified as a conservative.

Dos Passos' second trilogy, District of Columbia, was
as well received by conservatives as his U.S.A. had been by
liberals. The first volume, The Adventures of a Young Man,
published in 1939, traces the misfortunes of a young idealist,
Glen Spotswood. After coming under the influence of liberals
and communists at Columbia University, he goes west to work
with Chicano laborers. Driven out of his job by reactionary
elements of a Texas community, he returns to New York City,
where he affiliates with the Communist Party. The party
sends him to Kentucky to work with coal strikers, but he
soon finds that it really does not have the interests of the
miners at heart. So he goes to fight in Spain, only to be
imprisoned by the communists. He dies on a suicidal mission which he has agreed to take in order to get out of
prison.

But as the second volume of the series makes clear,
communists are not the only ones who exploit liberals' na-
ïveté. In Number One (1943) an American demagogue who
resembles Huey Long takes advantage of Tyler Spotswood,

brother of Glen who appeared in the previous novel.   But
Dos Passos does not blame demagoguery entirely on liberals;
he also indicts self-seeking businessmen and the common
people.

The concluding book of the trilogy, The Grand Design
(1949), deals with the failure of two more idealists, this
time two young men who join Franklin Roosevelt's New Deal
administration.   Millard Carroll and Paul Grove set out to
help make small farmers better able to cope with their problems without giving up independence.   Vicious, power-hungry
politicians and bureaucratic red tape make it impossible for
the protagonists to succeed and they resign in disgust.

Three years after completion of the District of Columbia, Dos Passos published Chosen Country.   In it he has Jay
Pignatelli, the central character, come to terms with twentieth-century American life without being misled or defeated.
A lawyer, Pignatelli, like many others of his generation,
goes to Europe to participate in World War I and remains
there after the war.   But he rejects Russian propaganda and
returns home to practice law.   Again, he does not allow himself to be used by the radicals.   The story ends with the
protagonist happily married and unequivocally committed to
the traditional American system.   In contrast to Dos Passos'
other novels, this one has a positive theme, a happy ending.

Dos Passos' next novel, Most Likely to Succeed (1954),
returns to a negative theme.   It traces the downfall of Jed
Morris, a dramatist whom fellow students had honored
with the accolade which provides the title for the book.
Again the villain is the Communist Party, which lures Morris into its sinister programs, destroys his love life, and
ruins his artistic career.

There still remained other institutions for Dos Passos

to treat.   In <u>The Great Days</u> (1958) he finds that the mass
media are a major threat to American values.   Using Roger
Thurloe, a military man who is hounded out of his office as
Secretary of Defense, and Roland Lancaster, a journalist who
has lost the popularity he once knew, Dos Passos demonstrates how a depersonalized "system" can destroy good men
by allowing the mass media to stir up popular opposition to
men whose opinions do not conform.   Thurloe, whose story
bears resemblances to that of James V. Forrestal, commits
suicide.   Lancaster does not, even though he finds nothing
that makes life appealing to him any longer.

In his final novel (1961) Dos Passos deals with individuals who are defeated by labor unions and financial manip-
ulators.   A group study, <u>Mid-century</u> describes Terry Bry-
ant's death at the hands of union-hired thugs, Frank Worthing-
ton's sell-out of his integrity to keep his union job, Jasper
Milliron's inability to follow sound business practices because
of interference by unwise investors, and gives accounts of
other decent men who find that bucking the system is a cost-
ly venture.

A basic question about Dos Passos is whether his
views changed over the years or whether he remained consistent in his basic philosophy and commitments.   The most
convincing interpretation is that he was never committed to
ideology but saw evils in the world and attacked them.   As
a young man he chose to attack injustices that were also
being attacked by Marxists.   For a time he undoubtedly felt
a kinship with revolutionary Marxism's promises of a new
world.   But with artistic success, acknowledgment by his
father, and the loss through execution by the communists of
a friend who was fighting for the Loyalists in Spain, Dos
Passos changed targets.   Rather than supporting the dispos-

sessed, Dos Passos chose to oppose the institutions that had
come to power as champions of the weak: the New Dealers,
labor bosses, and communists/fellow-travelers. Understandably such themes made him popular in right-wing circles. [8]

The reception of Taylor Caldwell by right-wing critics
is somewhat puzzling. By the mid-fifties her novels had
sold over seven million copies;[9] yet success, a National Review writer noted, had not dampened her "passionate faith in
America and in religion."[10] Her novel, The Devil's Advocate (not to be confused with a book by Morris West with the
same title), and other of her stories would seem to classify
her as an untainted rightist. She has publicly supported
right-of-center causes. [11] But except in American Opinion
circles her reception has not been as enthusiastic as that ac-
corded Allen Drury or John Dos Passos. Her strongly stated
view that war is the result of sinister plotting by international money interests and her fascination with nonchristian super-
naturalism (see her Dialogues with the Devil and The Search
for a Soul: Taylor Caldwell's Psychic Lives by Jess Stearn)[12]
likely explain at least part of her treatment by right-wing
critics.

Born in England, Caldwell, at six years of age, came
with her parents to the United States. From her autobio-
graphical statement, On Growing Up Tough (excerpts from
her contributions to American Opinion), it would appear that
she took seriously her father's statement upon sailing that
she was no longer a child. Even earlier, she reports, she
had learned that people who profess love for the unfortunate
are sentimental fakes. In American schools she found that
teachers reflected the sticky sentimentalism that she had
come to hate. Her most helpful education came from a few

years in the mountains of Kentucky, where her first husband
had gone to make his fortune.   She describes herself as a
pioneer wife who "roughed" it without complaint.   But she
left Kentucky (and her husband) to work in Buffalo, New York.
Eventually she became a successful writer, remarried, and
raised a family.

Of her many books (over thirty) three have been highly endorsed in right-wing circles because of what they say
about American social issues: The Devil's Advocate, Captains and Kings, and On Growing Up Tough.   The first two
are novels; the third is difficult to classify.

The Devil's Advocate, a futuristic, negative story, describes the demise and resurrection of American independence.
By the late part of the twentieth century, the nation is being
run by and for the advantage of three groups: governmental
bureaucrats, military men, and farmers.   Replacing the Constitution, "The Democracy," which began internationally with
the Bolshevik revolution in 1917 and gained a foothold in the
United States in the 1930s, has enslaved the masses of people.   The change has been made possible by fuzzy-thinking
intellectuals and sheep-like masses who let others think for
them.

But the darkest hour turns out to be just before day-
break.   Secretly, Minute Men have permeated the power
structure.   The Devil's Advocate focuses upon Andrew Durant,
a lawyer, who because of his loyalty and strength becomes a
major force in the Minute Men plan to alienate the elites so
that they will revolt.   As a regional commander, Durant
moves in on the farmers, withdrawing privileges that they
have accrued.   Surrounded by spies and potential entrapments,
Durant does his job well and eventually "the Democracy" is
repudiated, the Constitution restored.   Not all problems are

solved but the future is promising as the new leaders move
forward by moving backward to nineteenth century order of
things.

In contrast to The Devil's Advocate, Captains and
Kings is set in the past.   It traces the life of an Irish immigrant, Joseph Francis Xavier Armagh, who comes to the
United States before the American Civil War.   He makes a
fortune, establishes a family, and sets out to make his son
president of the United States.   The story is a brutal one,
with personal tragedies stalking Armagh in spite of his financial successes.   He provides for an orphaned brother and
sister but later repudiates them when the sister joins a con-
vent and the brother becomes a musician.   One son dies in
the Spanish-American War and a daughter receives brain
damage in a riding accident after she learns that the man
she wants to marry is really her uncle.   The second son,
who has made his bid for the presidency by entering several
state primary elections, dies at the hands of an extremist
before the national party convenes.   There are obvious parallels between the Armaghs and the Kennedys.   Except for
financial success, Armagh achievements do not rank high in
the author's treatment.

The lack of personal ethical conduct by the Armaghs
is only one part of the evil described in the novel.   They
own legislators, bribe judges, ignore rights of competitors,
and demand sacrifice of personal desires for the family interests.   But worse, the Armaghs are only one among an international society of moneyed families (the Committee for
Foreign Studies).   Ignoring national political machinery, the
elites determine the destiny of the world.   The American
Civil War and the upcoming World War I, as well as the approaching Russian Revolution, are small parts of the long-

ranged, carefully laid master plan that the group charts. Its
members care not for country, religion, or love. They as-
sassinate political leaders without hesitation. Lincoln, Gar-
field, and McKinley are only three of their victims. Young
Armagh's death results from his father's refusal to accept
the club's choice of Woodrow Wilson to become president in
1913. The academician is supposedly too naive and pliable
and hence susceptible to being used by the masters--to bring
about a federal income tax and a federal reserve system so
that all Americans might be enslaved.

If her novels were not enough to endear Taylor Caldwell to right-wingers, her articles in American Opinion solid-
ified the tie. On Growing Up Tough opens: "I began being
a conservative when I was very young." She denounces,
among other things, child lovers, unmanly men, liberated
women, hippies, and T. L. C. (Tender Loving Care).

According to Medford Evans, "Every normal, red-
blooded American likes Taylor Caldwell."[13] She was acclaimed in unqualified terms in one of his articles in American Opinion. In America's Future, Rosalie Gordon described
her work as "a reading experience of the highest order."[14]
National Review has not been as effusive as America's Future and American Opinion, but reviewers there have received her work enthusiastically. It has occasionally published an article by her or an excerpt from one of her books.

According to a writer in Intercollegiate Review, "no
single thinker has had the effect on ... the 'new intellectuals'
of the Right [that] has Ayn Rand."[15] And even though Whittaker Chambers denied that Rand should be considered a conservative, he recognized that "a great many of us dislike
much that Miss Rand dislikes."[16] Partly in response to

Chambers, E. Merrill Root argued that anyone who could
write as brilliantly as Rand could not really be an atheist.
He insisted that some of Howard Roark's ideas were "far
closer to theism--and to the rainbow mind of Christ--than
anything the National Council of Churches can ever con-
ceive. "[17] Garry Wills wrote a rejoinder to Root, insisting
that Rand was neither Christian nor conservative. [18] Several
readers joined the dialogue. A Connecticut minister apparently put an end to the argument; after pointing out that he
had not read Rand nor Root, he could see no reason to try
to resolve his ignorance until at least two letters to the
editor could agree on what either Rand or Root was saying. [19]

Rosalie Gordon, in America's Future, chose to ignore
Rand's unacceptable ideas and sympathize with the author because the New York Times had asked a woman who, Gordon
insisted, did not understand the book to review The Fountainhead upon its twenty-fifth anniversary. Since the review was
quite negative and since the writer did not admit that the
original review in the Times had been positive, Gordon was
incensed. Fortunately, she noted, the publisher of the novel
bought an advertisement in the Times and reprinted the original review. [20]

The nonreligious libertarians of the right view Rand
in a different light than do the theists. She has obviously
been able to verbalize clearly and admirably at least some
ideas that right-wingers appreciate. She does not build a
strong positive case but provides ammunition for use against
collectivists and humanitarians. Professor Root especially
appreciated her "brilliant skinning alive of all the phonies of
the earth. "[21]

It is not at all difficult to see why Rand would appeal
to right-wingers. We the Living, set in Russia, condemns

the Marxist state because it does not allow the individual to
live a free, dignified life. In the story a young woman dies
trying to free herself from her homeland after she becomes
disillusioned with the new order. In The Fountainhead Rand
creates an architect whose superiority is early-on made obvious to the reader but is not nearly so apparent to the "clods"
among whom he must live. In contrast to The Fountainhead,
Anthem and Atlas Shrugged are set in the future in unidenti-
fied lands. Both denounce mysticism and collectivism and
praise individualism. The symbolic dollar mark at the end
of Atlas Shrugged, although variously interpreted, can be
read as an unqualified endorsement of capitalism and materi-
alism. In her introduction to Calumet "K", Rand writes
that competence--a quality which in her understanding was
apparently more common in nineteenth-century America than
in the present--is the American characteristic which she has
tried to stress throughout her novels.

Whatever the problem with a label for Rand, a writer
in Human Events seems to have captured two basic points
concerning her works. First, her novels should be taken as
serious prophecy. Second, her "chief virtue is to see, and
emphasize, that the collectivist failure is a failure of the intellect. "23

Besides the four major figures, there are a number
of other novelists whose works have been published by conservative presses and endorsed by right-wing reviewers but
who have not been nearly as successful in the market place
as writers such as Drury. Although he has not been as
highly acclaimed as some other minor writers, no novelist
has made right-wing ideology more central in his work than
has Holmes Alexander.

Alexander is best known for his work as a syndicated newspaper columnist--but not "one of the kind Spiro Agnew blasts."24 Born in West Virginia in 1906, he has spent most of his life in the Maryland and the District of Columbia area. The son of an attorney, he grew up in an affluent, genteel society. At Princeton he was graduated with honors with a major in English. After teaching for a brief period, he was elected to the Maryland House of Delegates at the age of twenty-four. In 1935 he chose writing as a career and until World War II devoted himself to nonfiction--primarily American biography. In his autobiography he indicates that he aroused family displeasure by marrying a woman who did not measure up to the standards expected of him, even though his bride came from a family of "excellent Confederate blood."25

After serving in World War II as an air intelligence officer and pilot, he drifted into newspaper work upon returning to Washington. He wrote a political column which was distributed by the McNaught Syndicate. In his memoirs he describes himself as a maverick who alienated too many people in too many circles to be popularly known. After an unhappy experience with a brother over the settlement of their father's estate, Alexander wrote a novel (West of Washington) which painted some of his thinly-disguised relatives in a very unkind light. He subsequently found himself an outcast from the society in which he had grown up. As a columnist, he irritated conservatives by supporting President Truman's firing of General MacArthur. Liberals found him inconsistent because he endorsed Richard Nixon in 1960 after admitting that John Kennedy was better qualified to be president. But there are those who have honored Alexander. The University of West Virginia Library, which published his auto-

biography (Pen and Politics), has requested his papers. A
native of that state, he wrote a novel (Selina) which is set in
the area during the Civil War era.

Two of Alexander's novels treat American issues in
a manner that has won praise in right-wing circles. The
Spirit of '76: A Political Novel of the Near Future, published
by Arlington House, was selected and distributed by the Conservative Book Club. Equivocal Men: Tales of the Establishment was published by Western Islands Press, an affiliate
of the John Birch Society. Neither work has attracted critical interest; and even such conservative journals as the National Review gave them only slight treatment. Apparently
Senator Strom Thurmond's efforts in behalf of the book (described in the introduction) seem to have done little to draw
attention to The Spirit of '76.

In Equivocal Men (1964) Alexander acknowledges his
indebtedness to Allen Drury's Advise and Consent. He describes some of the observations that led him to write the
book:

> ... in the past twenty years America had declined
> from a world position of supremacy to one of no
> better than parity with its enemies, and that this
> descent had the nature of classic tragedy--the fall
> of a worthy being, not so much because of de-
> served punishment emanating from wickedness, but
> because of a fatal flaw in an otherwise good char-
> acter.... The people who were doing us in were
> the Equivocal Men. 26

Philip Obermeister, a young journalist, appears
throughout the book. He comes into contact with seven men
who reflect deadly equivocation. Obermeister romantically
pursues the wife of a scientist who defects to the Soviet
Union, only to see her take back her husband after a group
of American students rescues him from behind the Iron Cur-

tain--a place the scientist has found much less appealing than
the United States.

The first equivocal man, Calvin Borton, has emerged
as the most powerful liberal columnist in the nation.   Among
other things he believes that the time is overdue "for formally repealing the myth of nationalism, the ugly talk of racial
difference, the absurb sentimentality of patriotism."[27] Obermeister secures a job as an assistant to Borton, his ideal
columnist.   But soon he resigns in disgust, but not before
Borton has been made to realize that he has lost the power
to love--to love people and country.   He is left to agonize
over his dehumanization when Obermeister will not remain
to save him.

The equivocal man of means is a Cyrus Eaton type of
wealthy person who repudiates nationalism in the interest of
globalism.   By stealth Obermeister attends a conference
called by Hiram Hewlet to bring together American and Russian scientists who hopefully can work around national bar-
riers to international brotherhood.   To his dismay Obermeister sees that the Americans are outsmarted by the
trained Soviet propagandists and is even more dismayed to
learn that his reports have not made the papers at home.
Rather, Calvin Borton's columns, relying upon information
from Hewlet, have made the conference sound noble.   So
Hewlet is allowed to continue his damaging practices.

A third part of the book focuses upon Beeline Buckler,
who is anything but equivocal as he overwhelms the communists in Berlin.   He ignores air corridor restrictions and
wall guards.   After the mayor of East Berlin flees because
he fears what Buckler is trying to do, the patriotic general's
work is undone when equivocal leaders in Washington have
him arrested and replaced.

So goes the equivocation through four other chapters.
A man of learning, Bors Dvorska, is confirmed for an important advisory post in the national executive administration,
while a senator who objects to him because of the scholar's
attitude toward use of atomic weapons is defeated in the next
primary. Miles Fleetwood--son of a labor union czar--who
fled the country rather than fight in Korea, returns home
after years of roaming on the expense account of Hiram Hewlet. After Phil Obermeister exposes Fleetwood's growing
power behind the scenes in Washington, Fleetwood commits
suicide when he realizes that he is nothing but a man of
emptiness. Another equivocating intellectual, Robert Lamb-
right Poindexter, is made Secretary of State, but as a result
of Obermeister's influence, tries to avoid giving up all his
integrity by having a homosexual brother-in-law of the editor
of the Washington Standard arrested for being a communist
courier. Finally, Mark O'Malley, a rugged, gambling capi-
talist, is defeated in his efforts to take over a sky boat project which the federal government is dropping after years of
financing. O'Malley is opposed by Senator Whipperpool, who
objects to the capitalistic notion of making a profit on such
a project.

The Spirit of '76 concerns the emergence of a modern
George Washington who in a single year puts the American
house in order. In a plane crash, Samuel Tilden Lepol
(rhymes with people), a popular Republican president committed to "egalitarianism, globalism, and electoral major-
ities," is killed. His successor, Jerry Chase, a Virginia
lawyer who before becoming a Senator had been willing to defend only wealthy clients, is attending a conference in South
America at the time of the president's death. Acting on un-
substantiated information, Calvin Borton, a liberal columnist,

reports in print that Miles Standish Smith, president of the
Nathan Hale Society, piloted the plane that brought down the
presidential craft.   Philip Obermeister, a conservative columnist, reports that it was Carlos Martinez, a black Puerto
Rican communist who has given the name of Attorney General Erasmus Hannibal, also black, as the person to be noti-
fied in case of emergency.   Eula Breck, another reporter,
finds Martinez, who has parachuted to the ground after ram-
ming FAA One with his National Guard jet.   He tells Breck
that he has done so to clear the way for Hannibal to become
president.

The story then develops three strands: the actions of
the new president, the shenanigans of two matriarch-dom-
inated families which seek to wrest the presidency from
Chase, and the fortunes and misfortunes of the three journalists.   President Chase addresses American citizens by
television from South America, telling them that he will continue his diplomatic work before returning home.   By courier he nominates a hawkish general to be the new vice president, asks for the resignation of all cabinet members except
the attorney general, and then turns to Latin American diplomacy.   Bluntly he denounces collective ventures, asserting
that any nation that wants American aid will have to sign a
bilateral treaty which provides for security.   When the dic-
tator of El Salvador is unseated by a popular uprising, American troops immediately restore him and then invade Cuba,
which is blamed for the unrest in El Salvador.   President
Chase flies the first of the bomber planes which pave the
way for a landing force in Cuba.

China is put in its place by a manned satellite which,
armed with atomic weapons, stands poised to reduce China to
ruins.   The president asks a powerful man in the ruling hier-

archy in the U.S.S.R., a man with whom the new president
has had encounters around hunting circles in Maryland when
both were young men, to meet him secretly for a summit
conference at sea. The president arrives unshaven in a
rumpled pilot's uniform. In no uncertain terms, he warns
the Russian leader that a new day has dawned in American
diplomacy and cautions the communist leader not to provoke
the United States into a nuclear showdown because, since
death is preferable to fear, the United States will not hesitate
to resort to any force available to assert its will.

Having acted decisively to untangle diplomacy, the
president turns to domestic problems. He soon alienates
Congress because of his economic austerity and attention to
the Constitution. Soon the House of Representatives votes
for impeachment on charges that the president has failed to
respect the dignity of Congress. The Senate, though, fails
to convict. Meanwhile, the communists, in cahoots with columnist Borton, have stirred up mass protests. When protesters crash through the White House fence and encamp on
the lawn, the president again takes to his plane and drops
subfatal nerve gas into the crowds. He has been angered because the protesters have so intimidated his wife that she had
had to be hospitalized with a nervous disorder.

Soon the president again has masses of people feeling
proud to be Americans. In less than a year he has so re-
arranged things that Republicans are sure to gain a congressional majority for the first time in decades. No one could
come close to unseating Chase, but surprisingly he steps
aside, much to the dismay of American voters. His primary
interest is to restore to health his frail wife. In November
the country is put into the hands of a manly Republican majority and a safe president, so all is rosy.

One task that President Chase especially relishes is
putting in their places the two wealthy families which are
competing to become ruling dynasties.   Juno Lepol, theatri-
cal wife of the slain former president, seeks to replace
Chase with her son, Dwight D. Lepol.   At first she refuses
to move from the White House, then she works to bring on
the impeachment charges.   But she carelessly falls into a
trap set by President Chase and is left powerless.   In disgust, Juno Lepol changes parties, hoping to combine forces
with other malcontents to dethrone Chase.   But the Democratic Finnegans, who hold a Senate seat and governorship,
are unable, even with Lepol's help, to outdo Chase.

Two of the three journalists in the story find new life
through President Chase.   Conservative Obermeister not only
covers dramatic events of the new administration; he wins
the love of Chi Chi Chase, daughter of the president and a
successful actress who has joined the Chastity Club.   Obermeister first seeks to win journalist Eula Breck, who for
the first time was tempted to give up her membership in the
Virgins Club for him.   But he loses her when she finds another woman in his apartment when she comes to announce
her decision.   But with her aid, Obermeister is later able to
demonstrate to a court of law that he has not slandered Seth
Phillipson, Secretary of Peace under President Lepol, whom
he has called a communist.   The judge ends the case by proclaiming:

> Let it go forth from this time and place that a new
> hour of freedom has dawned.   Next time a conscien-
> tious newspaperman finds a Communist, let him
> speak out loud and clear without fear of reprisal. [28]

Breck happily turns her energies to writing a history of
Chase's life and work, while Obermeister and Chi Chi go their
happy way.

But no happy fate awaits Calvin Borton. Even though
Miles Standish Smith offers to drop a libel suit if Barton will
apologize for reporting that Smith assassinated Lepol, Borton
finds himself unable to apologize to a "kook." He is given
a symbolic one-day jail sentence. To make his humiliation
more complete, Smith is offered a post in Chase's administration while the liberal columnist is left to endure his agony
in isolation, a fate made worse by a noble deathbed statement left by Smith, who dies a few days after the trial.
But, motivated by love, Borton's secretary accepts the challenge of humanizing the man who, in forgetting what it means
to be an American, loses far more than his patriotism.

As Alexander has pointed out in his memoirs, he is
not without critics among right-wing spokesmen. Medford
Evans, after carefully pointing out that his is a positive rather than a negative review of one of Alexander's books, noted
that the only rationale for a conservative to support Truman
rather than MacArthur was "the purpose of proving independence."[29] Generally, though, Alexander's fiction has been
received favorably in right-wing circles, primarily because
of content rather than artistic merit. After reading Equivocal Men, W. F. Rickenbacker wondered if Alexander might
have "a novel up his sleeve about a millionaire clerk to a
certain Democratic Senate majority leader."[30] E. Merrill
Root described him as "an erudite, sound historian,"[31] while
M. Stanton Evans reacted positively to his ability to combine
"fact, futuristic fantasy, and right-wing doctrine."[32] He
also appreciated Alexander's ability to parody the "liberal
no-think."[33] F. Farr has described Alexander as an "all-
around literary man" with a "sure, professional touch in the
writing of fiction."[34]

Finis Farr, whose work has appeared in National Review and occasionally in mass circulation magazines, has written several biographical studies, including as subjects Frank Lloyd Wright, Jack Johnson, and Margaret Mitchell. In 1967 Arlington House published his first novel, The Elephant Valley, "a spy novel in which the Americans are NOT the villains. "[35]

The story goes that on the basis of an unwarranted recommendation by a psychiatrist--who wears "rimless glasses and instead of regular socks ... socklets that barely cover his ankles, and one of those metallic suits, and a huge metal clasp on his tie"[36]--David Bell, a "born gentleman," is reassigned from Washington to New York by the Company (an organization which resembles the C. I. A.). Eventually the agent realizes that he has been put into a valley where old elephants go to die. But on the surface Bell has been given a meaningless job of penetrating the organization of Jefferson Kane, a millionaire who has been taken in by the Soviet Union, which uses Kane's Foundation as a part of its international power network. Bell takes his work seriously and learns that Kane, cooperating with a Nobel prize-winning British scientist, is planning to be part of a major plot by the communists to destroy a nuclear plant in the United States and start World War III. Despite Gestapo-like efforts on the part of some of Kane's affiliates, Bell is able to convince his superiors in Washington that a dangerous plot is afoot. Eventually the communists are defeated and Bell is reinstated to his former position.

In the novel one learns that American foundations (educational, humanitarian funds that are provided by American businessmen who have become wealthy) support leftist rather than patriotic causes. [37] That Robert Kennedy resembles "a

juvenile delinquent explaining a rumble to a parole officer. "[38]
That American intellectuals are as uncritical of a Bertram
Russell type of pacifist as were the cultists who gathered
around "fiddle-scraping, poodle-haired old Dr. Einstein. "[39]
According to the biographical sketch on the book cover, the
author served as an intelligence officer "in Washington and
elsewhere from 1950 to 1955. " P. L. Buckley admitted in
National Review that the plot is unclear but that even so the
story is gripping and that the protagonists are people a reader cares about. [40] Rosalie Gordon believed that Farr's novel
had "what so many popular spy stories lack, the ring of au-
thenticity, no doubt because Finis Farr spent five years as
an intelligence officer. "[41]

Other presses also brought out spy stories. In 1963,
the Devin-Adair Company published David O. Woodbury's
Five Days to Oblivion. The author, who became a regular
contributor to American Opinion and who has published over
fifteen books on scientific subjects, builds his story around
a Russian scheme to abduct outstanding American scientists.
The protagonist, Sam Bowden, disappears while on a vacation
in Maine. He is tricked by a fellow scientist who works for
the federal government but who is also part of the Soviet
espionage system. The governmental agencies prove so inept
that Bowden's boss (a university dean) and an ethical F. B. I.
man take it upon themselves to rescue the kidnapped Bowden.
Little by little they untangle the mystery and eventually convince government intelligence leaders that they are correct
about the kidnapping. But to the dismay of the sleuths, representatives of the State Department step in and insist that
they have known of the case all along; they insist further that
the diplomatic corps has priority in handling the matter.

Stymied by the diplomats, the dean and lawman enlist the aid
of a newspaperman who is able to work around bureaucratic
blocks.   Meanwhile, Bowden has not been inactive.   In a dar-
ing gamble, he sets fire to the house in which he is being
held captive and draws the attention of his would-be rescuers
to the island where he is captive.   At the last moment Bowden is rescued and returns to work on missile research.

Throughout the book the reader is told of "the collapse of the American will," the "subjugation to the will of
the enemy--permanently," "the skillful eroding of the independence of Americans over the past few years," and the
"softening process, going on in every city and hamlet in the
country."[42]   The traitor in the book reminds his captive
that governmental departments "are very cooperative [in subversive plots] ... State, particularly."[43]   As in other such
novels, intellectuals "for some idiotic reason" seem to be
"the easiest guy[s] in the world to brainwash and send wool-
gathering."[44]   But then there are a few decent Americans
who "don't come easy," who are not the "dupes" the Russians
have found in other countries."[45]

In her review of Five Days to Oblivion, Rosalie Gordon noted that the tale is "close enough to possible reality to
scare or shock the mystery fan into muttering 'it could happen.'"[46]   But she also admitted that the author stretched
"the long arm of coincidence almost to the breaking point."[47]
She reported that Mr. Faraday's Formula, Woodbury's second
spy novel, is even better than his first.   The story continues
the dean-F.B.I. man coalition into new adventures.[48]   The
story concerns a young scientist who "succeeds in defying the
law of gravity" in the presence of an exchange student who is
really a Russian spy.   The rescue of the scientist from his
communist kidnappers provides the tension in the book.[49]

Woodbury's third novel, <u>You're Next on the List</u>, concerns an attempt by a government agency (Office of Home
Advisory on Human Affairs--OHAHA) to add a tranquilizing
chemical to the water supply of a Boston suburb. The goal
of Aphrodisia Kince, bureaucrat in charge of the project, is
to neutralize "crackpot rightists" who have been too verbal
in their objections to government policies. But again Dean
George Riam, this time without the aid of the F.B.I. agent,
rises to defeat Washington's scheme. Using town meetings
as his forum he eventually overcomes citizens' indifference
and preserves their freedom. 50

Even the Pentagon appears to have been taken over by
subversives in a novel written under the pseudonym of Victor J. Fox. According to <u>The Pentagon Case,</u> 51 persons in
sensitive posts in the armed forces have subtly chosen psychological devices to demoralize military men. The proof
is the rapidly declining reenlistment rates in the three
branches of military service. The problem is diagnosed by
Brett Cable, an experienced public relations man who is
hired by J. Hardy Wells, Assistant Secretary of Defense for
Military Morale, to do something to stop the decline. Cable
discovers that even the Pentagon is decorated with pictures
which show only the negative side of military service--Amer-
icans wounded, Americans dead, Americans defeated rather
than the sinking of enemy ships, the shooting down of enemy
planes.

Expanding his investigation, Cable learns that negativ-
ism fills treatments of the military in magazines, in movies,
and in religious conferences. Soon he develops an airtight
case which proves that key persons in the Pentagon are not
only approving, but are encouraging the distribution of anti-

military propaganda.   He concludes that the Russians have
chosen to work in this indirect way rather than engage the
nation in a shooting war.   And to Cable's dismay, he sees
how successful they have been.   To his further dismay and
even to his defeat, he finds that his discoveries are repudiated.   No one will believe him--he almost ends up in a mental hospital because he tries to work around bureaucratic red
tape.   He leaves government service with plans to go to the
people--by writing novels under the pen name of Victor J.
Fox.

Another novel exposes why the executive and legisla-
tive branches of government are unable to act effectively
against sinister forces.   In 1968, Stephen C. Shadegg, who
was Barry Goldwater's "political manager" from 1952 to 1962,
published The Remnant, a story of a noble, one-term Democratic New Mexico senator.   The plot traces the efforts of
Calvin Fessenden to have a Senate committee investigate
charges of criminal activities by an east coast labor leader.
The cowman-pilot-senator finds that the leadership of his
party resorts to illegal, unethical activities in trying to block
his investigation.   Understandably union leadership opposes
him, but the senator is overwhelmed when he learns that the
management of the automobile industry also opposes the investigation because it fears a general strike.   The senator's
apartment is bugged and his friends fear that his life is in
danger.   But Fessenden refuses to give in and forces the
Senate to act on his charges.   He announces that he will not
seek reelection as planned, lest he be a problem for his
party or that it appear that he is merely trying to find an
issue upon which to base his bid for reelection.

Contrary to expectations, the senator's action works

for the welfare of the nation. One union votes to strike, but others do not. The popularity of the senator's acts demonstrate to compromised politicians that voters do care about integrity. Even Fessenden's wife is motivated to give up addiction to alcohol; the senator gives up his Chicana mistress on the ranch in New Mexico. His daughter, referring to her study of western civilization, points out that "God always reserves a remnant to do His work.... Dad's one of those men, and there aren't very many, who still believe."[52] Rosalie Gordon referred to Isaiah's assertion that except for the remnant, "we should have been as Sodom, and we should have been like unto Gomorrah."[53]

One who knows of Senator Goldwater's political speeches in the 1964 presidential campaign will not be surprised by the ideas of Senator Fessenden. He believes that "no one wanted to do anything for himself anymore."[54] He opposes the welfare state and big government.[55] He also believes that the dispossessed could secure an abundant life in the United States if they were only motivated to do so. He sees his mission, not to reform the country, but to save it.[56]

The United States is not the only endangered nation. When the Kissing Had to Stop is set in England. Written by Constantine FitzGibbon, an "American living in Ireland," who served as an intelligence officer in World War II, the book was first published in 1960. In 1972 Arlington House republished it and made it available through the Conservative Book Club. Like other rightist novels it portrays what could happen if Westerners take Soviet disarmament propaganda seriously.

Working through subversive and self-serving politicians, the Soviet Union indirectly brings about the dissolution of

Parliament and a general election. Surprisingly, the Labour
Party wins an uncontested majority by making disarmament
and withdrawal of American troops from England the major
issues. No sooner are the bases closed than the Russians
send in "inspection teams" which take over the nation. The
persons who were duped into cooperating with the communists
end up tortured to death or in Siberian labor camps. Threatened with a war with China and having been rudely asked to
leave England, the United States can only sit by and watch
the misled nation be enslaved. The only hope lies in a band
of guerrilla forces which have not surrendered. The romance
has gone from the lives of the foolish politicians, intellectuals,
and artists who have betrayed their nation.

Grace Lumpkin writes not of what might happen in the
future but about what took place in the United States in the
past. Like Whittaker Chambers, whom she describes as a
longtime friend, Lumpkin repudiated her association with
communism for a deep religious faith. Earlier she received
a Marxist award for her proletarian novel, To Make My
Bread, and an O. Henry award for "The Treasure," a short
story. In 1962, the John Birch Society publishing house published Full Circle, a fictional account of her life.

Full Circle traces the narrator's spiritual journeys.
Following the traumatic shock which results when her liberal
minister-husband chooses to divorce her and leave the ministry for another woman, the narrator is drawn into communist circles by her daughter, who has been attracted to
the group because of its civil rights activities. The daughter
joins the Communist Party and rises rapidly to a responsible
leadership job. Both mother and daughter find their new
world a rewarding one and feel secure and appreciated. But

then something happens. For some poorly explained reasons, the communists replace the daughter and expel her from the party. After the daughter goes into a catatonic state the mother takes her home to recuperate. In anger and disgust the mother repudiates her faith in the party and in desperation turns back to the church. The story ends with the penitent father back home and the daughter on the way to recovery--thanks in part to the efforts of a young Christian man.

Backward-looking novels are rarer than future-oriented ones. In right-wing periodicals, no novel has been better received than The Journal of David Q. Little, a first novel by R. Daniel McMichael, a forty-two year-old public relations man. Published by Arlington House and offered free with membership in the Conservative Book Club, it was also offered free with a subscription to America's Future. Without exception reviewers in right-wing periodicals praised the book in exalted terms. They welcomed the book as an alternative to On the Beach and other stories which exploited the possibility of a nuclear holocaust. Right-wing critics recognized the propaganda value of Seven Days in May and Dr. Strangelove for the liberal cause and believed that they finally had found a book which focused upon other dangers--threats "equally horrible and much more real. "57 Rather than military weapons, they believed that moral relativism and civil indifference were the major problems. And in contrast to other scare books, this one was described as realistic--not what could happen, but what is happening. Whereas George Orwell's 1984 was set far into the future (when it was written) and in a foreign land, The Journal of David Q. Little, though far-fetched, concerns the American present.

The journal, as the author introduces it, is discovered by a group of Australian scientists who come to North America in the year 2223. They locate the diary in a former Christian mission in what was once the western United States. The record describes the fate of a cross-section of Americans when the World Order of Nations (WON--which turns out to be another name for the Russian Empire) set up a nation-wide organization to "enforce" the Joint Treaty of Friendship which has been signed by the United States and the U.S.S.R. as a peaceful alternative to a threatened nuclear holocaust.

David Quincy Little, the journalist, is a happily married, middle class steel salesman, the descendant of a nineteenth-century rugged individualist. Committed to the American system, he is one of the few Americans who immediately see through the sham of what is transpiring. Even his wife falls for the party line, his children turn against him, and he eventually resorts to begging. He and a small number of other Americans from various segments of the society form a commune of the dispossessed in a forsaken barge. Their downfall represents the downfall of the American way of life. Eventually, in some unexplained way, the small band of believers drifts downriver and moves west. From their nuclear community grows a resistance movement which ultimately prevails over the Russianized system.

On at least one occasion a novel published by a conservative press was later brought out by a mainstream house. In 1965 the Henry Regnery Company published <u>Man in the Mirror</u> by Frederick Ayers, Jr., an ex-F.B.I. agent. [58] Signet Books later published a paperback edition of the book. It is a far-fetched tale about Soviet espionage in the United States. In brutal fashion communist intelligence agents

choose a former Nazi who fled to Argentina after World War
II and give him a choice of cooperating or being turned over
to Israelis.   They choose him because he looks like Roger
Lowell Storrow, a highly-placed adviser on security matters
to the American president.   When Storrow goes to Mexico
for a vacation, Russian agents kidnap him, have his wife
killed in an automobile accident, and send their well-prepared
agent to play Storrow.   Almost everyone is taken in--but not
quite.   One person begins to follow up his suspicions in spite
of discouraging red tape responses from Washington bureaucrats.   Meanwhile, Storrow escapes by making a bomb from
aluminum cigar wrappers.   He again falls into communist
hands but is rescued just in time by the combined efforts of
the CIA and an attractive Mexican actress with whom Storrow
has had a brief affair.   His replacement has been told to
leave a small fusion bomb at a meeting of the National Security Council, to wipe out the top leadership of the United
States.   But at the last moment he realizes that he is a lost
man and refuses to follow his instructions.   He dies in a
blast that was meant to kill security council members.

Occasionally mainstream presses publish a novel
which wins the praise of right-wing critics.   When the Conservative Book Club announced its inauguration in 1964, it
listed The Big Man by Henry J. Taylor as the type of novel
it would try to distribute. 59   A month earlier Ralph de Toledano had been complimentary toward the book, after noting
that he looked upon the author as "an old friend who has
stood like Horatius at the bridge in defense of those conservative ideals which sustain me. "60   He also noted that the
theme was "one of transcendent importance in this year of
our Lord 1964. "

The "big man" of Taylor's novel impressed de Toledano as a composite of Wendell Willkie and of his Republican
opponents. 61 A lawyer in a small town in Illinois, Frank
Killory comes to the attention of a major New York City law
firm when he wins a hopeless case for a local automobile
dealer against United Motors. A Lincolnesque figure, Killory joins the New York firm and soon is recognized across
the land as a first-rate courtroom attorney. Eventually he
is persuaded to become a candidate for the presidency. In-
fluential, admirable (conservative) men around the country
come to his support when they see what a decent sort he is.
But he also attracts others--men who put power above princi-
ple--who do him in. Rather than staying with his early
stated conservative platform, Killory switches to the liberals'
line. Being wise and principled, his original supporters withdraw their support and the compromised candidate is left to
face defeat at the upcoming convention.

In D. Keith Mano, at least one reviewer believed that
the conservative camp had found its Hemingway. In 1970
Jeffrey Hart wrote:

> Please, NR readers, remember that I told
> you so. You have the opportunity now to witness
> the emergence of a novelist of the first magnitude;
> you can be in the position of the reader who in
> 1926 picked up a thin volume off the counter and
> began to read: 'Robert Cohn was once....' An
> entire new imaginative world comes into existence.
> And now Keith Mano, who has just published his
> third novel, and is still under thirty, comes for-
> ward as a comparable force.... 62

Whether or not Mano can measure up to such expectations remains to be seen. But his novels have been received positively in mainstream as well as rightist circles,

even though his books have not become best-sellers.   He
sometimes writes and reviews for such mass media as the
New York Times.   In a brief biographical sketch, Lewis
Nichols has described Mano as a businessman-writer.   According to Nichols, Mano, a man who really wanted to be an
actor, got into writing "more or less by accident."   Upon the
death of his father, Mano took over the X-Pando Corporation
(maker of a cement product) and took up writing on the side.
An Episcopalian, he has set out to write eight novels which
deal with "traditional Christianity in the modern world."
With a smile he accepts a description of himself as a "Christian pornographer."[63]

His first four novels have especially appealed to Jeffrey Hart.   As described by Hart, Bishop's Progress deals
with a "John Robinson dishonest-to-God type of modern bishop who learns that there are more things in heaven and
earth than are dreamt of by Harvey Cox."[64]

Horn, Mano's second novel, concerns a white priest
who goes to Harlem to take charge of a hopelessly run-down
church.   His neighbor, Horn, is a grotesque boxer who has
an unusual deformity, a single horn-like protrusion on the
top of his head.   The unusual man has characteristics of
Muhammed Ali (verbal, champion boxer) and Malcolm X
(leader of militant anti-christian, anti-white black sect).
Acting the role of an illiterate, Horn seems to hate cauca-
sians as well as their values and customs.   Yet he is taken
by the saintly white priest, who offers a complete contrast
to the role-playing, liberal white priest whom Horn has been
using.   Eventually, it is made known that Horn is really a
devotee of Western art and literature.   Indeed, he has built
up a secret apartment in the basement of the white priest's
church which has a tunnel connecting it with Horn's building.

Just before he goes out to be killed by militant blacks who
have taken over his following, Horn admits to the white priest
his respect for Christianity.

Mano's third novel, War Is Heaven! (1970) is set in
Camaguay, a Central American nation that is in the throes
of a national liberation uprising.   The story describes a joint
American-Camaguyan mission to deliver medical supplies to
a rendezvous point on Lake Negro.   The group is composed
of men from quite varied backgrounds.   The major part of
the story has to do with the tension between Andrew Jones,
a black, cowardly Navy corpsman, and Sergeant Clarence
Hook, a fearless, mystical, white American who sees visions
and who believes that he has supernatural ability.   The squad
marches through villages that have been wiped out by the
enemy Riffs, survives an ambush, and endures debilitating
physical suffering while crossing tropical jungles.   One member of the group turns out to be a double agent who ab-
sconds with the radio.   After three days of waiting the squad
starts back to base camp, unable to deliver the supplies.
But during the wait, Hook and Jones keep up their contest of
wills.   Hook is wounded by an enemy mine and dies after a
lengthy engagement with the black corpsman about their con-
flicting values.

As interpreted by Hart, the book has to do with "existence itself. " It demonstrates that "teeming life exists only
where there is teeming death, " and that, although war is hell,
it is also heaven--"because, qualitatively, war is no different
from existence itself. " Since the issues must be faced "they
might as well be faced in Camaguay [Vietnam?] as anywhere
else. "65

In 1971 Mano published The Death and Life of Harry
Goth, his fourth novel in four years.   Well received by re-

viewers in places such as the New York Times Book Review[66] and Newsweek, [67] the book also received praise from Hart: "The Death and Life of Harry Goth is at once the funniest and most moving thing that I have ever read.... No one who reads this novel can doubt that Keith Mano is the best American novelist writing at the present time."[68]

As described by reviewers, the black comedy novel is the story of Harry Goth and his family, the members of which form a microcosm of humanity. Married to a female race car driver who dominates him, Goth is told that he is to die from leukemia. But he does not. Rather he is involved in three other funerals. Underneath the comical surface, the book deals with serious philosophical questions.

Mano's fifth novel, The Proselytizer, which describes an evangelist who seduces women and then converts them, received less enthusiastic treatment than his previous ones. [69] His sixth novel, published the next year, has to do with the ecology movement. The Bridge, a pessimistic, futuristic story, takes the ecology movement to an absurd future stage: no life, except human, can be destroyed. People live on inorganic diets. Eventually the decision is made that all people must commit suicide because breathing, a process which cannot be altered, destroys life. The mass suicide is foiled by one man, but the restructured society is far from admirable.

Like The Proselytizer, this book was not as enthusiastically received as Mano's earlier ones. In National Review, Patricia S. Coyne (rather than Jeffrey Hart, who had treated Mano's other books) praised the style but reacted negatively to the content. She objected to the excessive premise and the inadequate theology. [70] But Mano is obviously still appreciated; as a contributing editor of National

<u>Review</u> he writes a regular column, "The Gimlet Eye."

Many books have focused upon international dealings of the U.S.S.R. without earning right-wing labels for their authors. For example, Ian Fleming's James Bond stories have appealed to a broad spectrum of readers but he made no special overtures to right-wing groups nor did such groups attempt to identify the author as one of theirs, for obvious reasons. But a number of books have registered well among right-wing reviewers and have been boosted by conservative groups. <u>The First Team</u>, by John Ball, who also wrote <u>In the Heat of the Night</u>, is one such book.

The First Team has to do with a small group of Americans who undo the Soviet conquest of the United States. By some unexplained method and for some unexplained purpose, Russian forces take over the United States without a war. They begin by occupying key leadership posts--political and industrial. On the surface it seems that the populace has submitted without turning to rebellion. While not enthusiastic about the new order, they have no desire to resist.

But unknown to Americans and Russians, a team of experts has been designated and equipped, by a president who foresaw the eventuality, to overthrow the occupation. Led by a former Chief of Naval Operations, Admiral Haymarket--who has been one of the few men who could put Senator Fitzhugh of the Foreign Relations Committee in his place --the team stealthily takes over a new nuclear submarine that is loaded with enough missiles to destroy the world. After Senator Fitzhugh's son is murdered by Russian occupation forces, the senator joins efforts with the underground crew to bring an end to Russian occupation, a job which has been made easier by an unstable leadership in Russia. There are

references to an insensitive Congress which has weakened
the military forces through budget cuts over the years, national leaders who are too naive to see the Soviet threat,
and a citizenry which has little will to fight--all of which
leads rightists to insist that the book is not fantasy. [71]

Another book which fits into the same category is
The Tashkent Crisis by William Craig. By the author of
The Fall of Japan, a nonfiction study, the novel concerns the
reaction of the American leadership to an ultimatum for un-
conditional surrender by the Russians who have developed--
and tested on a forest in Siberia and on a nuclear plant in
Israel--a laser weapon by which whole cities in any part of
the world can be destroyed from the Soviet Union without the
deployment of weapons or troops. As in The First Team,
despite congressional cuts of budgets which have weakened
the armed forces, a small group of persons are chosen by
the president, upon the recommendation of his intelligence
and military advisers, to take a small hydrogen bomb to the
Tashkent area to destroy the laser machine. The team is
captured, thanks in part to a spy among its membership, but
a Russian scientist destroys the plant when he realizes that
a madman is in control of the Kremlin. His act aborted another American project, which was to drop atomic weapons
on the base from the air. When the planes turn back, new
leaders take over in Moscow and all-out war is averted.
Rosalie Gordon reacted by insisting that the author "manages
to achieve a startling real reality without resort to the bath-
room or the bedroom. "[72]

In right-wing fiction, the white South usually receives
sympathetic treatment. Southerners are mainstays of many
of the right-wing causes. And even though the best known

southern writers--such as William Faulkner, Robert Penn
Warren, and Tennessee Williams--are not known as apologists
for the South, other writers have written positively of the
heritage. One such man, John O. Beaty, a long-time professor of English at Southern Methodist University, has vigor-
ously defended the Anglo-Saxon tradition, both in his novels
and his nonfiction. His Swords in the Dawn, an historical
novel, glorifies "the first Englishmen. " In Image of Life,
he denounces the "decadent sentimentalism" of modern literature and urges a return to the Anglo-Saxon tradition. In the
early 1950s he became the center of a controversy when he
protested against the growing presence of nonchristians (Jews)
among the faculty at Southern Methodist University. His anticommunist book, The Iron Curtain Over America, also generated criticism. George E. Sokolsky, for example, took
Beaty to task for implying that communism is a Jewish movement. 73

     In Crossroads (1956) Beaty set out to portray the no-
bility of the Southern way of life. Set in Virginia in the
late 1930s, the story follows the courtship and marriage of
an humble, aristocratic young man, Allen Mansfield. At
first he regards a local girl as a likely choice for a wife.
But when she lies to him and goes to a local dance hall, he
becomes disillusioned with her. Besides that, he cannot appreciate her family's taking in tourists in an effort to make
money. But one of the tourists is a Canadian girl, Eliza-
beth Campbell, who catches Mansfield's fancy. Conversations
between the two and among members of the two families explain the nobility of Virginia life. The Canadians have a
great number of questions about the treatment of blacks, but
they come to see the wisdom of segregation. It turns out
that the Canadians are descendants of Loyalists--from the

same area of Virginia--who fled northward in the American
Revolution. So the Anglo-Saxon line is reinvigorated with the
infusion of untainted blood. The book is a glowing tribute
to WASP people and institutions as well as agrarian values.
In National Review, Revilo Oliver described the characters
as people of fundamental decency:

> ... two heroines, although they can read and have
> passed puberty, are virgins unsaved by Freud, and
> the most prominent young man in the story not only
> respects his grandfather but even comes to accept
> wholeheartedly the Southern traditions of his fam-
> ily. 74

Humor is not a major facet of conservative literature.
In Al Capp, conservatives thought they had found a counterpart of the liberals' Herblock. Capp's Hardhat's Bedtime
Story Book was especially well received. Occasionally other
light books in a humorous vein--such as Turnip Greens and
Sergeant Stripes by Martin Grimes, The Patent Leather Stomp-
ing Shoes by Lucille Hooper, and The Ass That Went to Washington by George Koether--were published by Arlington House
or Caxton Press. Reviewers liked Leopold Tyrmand's The
Rosa Luxemburg Contraceptives Cooperative: A Primer in
Communist Civilization (published by Macmillan) but the reviewer in American Opinion was suspicious:

> He [Tyrmand] writes a wonderful antiCommunist
> line, but since coming to the United States in 1966
> he has been a Ford Foundation Fellow and written
> for The Reporter and The New Yorker ... some-
> body is fooling somebody. 75

An I. O. U. for Emily by Lu Gene Weldon is one humorous story which right-wingers found worthy as entertain-
ment and as social comment. In the story, Emily Parson,
who has just won a lucrative settlement in a lawsuit which

her attorney had insisted she would never win, chooses to
demonstrate that the federal government can be defeated also.
Objecting to income tax deductions as unconstitutional and to
the assigning of social security numbers as dehumanizing,
she persuades the citizens of La Honda, California, to close
their bank accounts and do business through letters of credit.
Outwitted, Internal Revenue Service agents lay siege to the
town, surrounding it with armed troops. Emily is eventually
arrested, but not before she has won converts to her simple
notions: the social security must be abolished and the income tax reconsidered. As she goes to prison, other persons begin a national campaign to collect a hundred million
signatures to request a return to the Constitution of 1788 and
the first ten amendments. The reviewer in America's Future evidently did not take the proposed cutting of the constitution back quite so far--she suggested that Emily "believes
in the ... pre-New Deal Constitution. "[76]

       Most conservative fiction was published by the larger
publishing houses in the right-wing such as Caxton, Devin-
Adair, and Arlington. On the fringes of the camp an occa-
sional book appeared from other sources. Because of the
author's apparent resources to produce and distribute the
book, H. L. Hunt's Alpaca Revisited became fairly well-
known, at least by title. So much of the book is devoted to
a discussion of the technical provisions of an ideal constitution for the country of Alpaca that the story line is almost
nonexistent. A young man, Juan Achala, sets out from Alpaca, his native land, to learn about the best type of government. In the process he meets a young opera singer, Mara
Hani, who becomes his wife. But Achala seems to be far
more concerned with political matters than with romance.

He surrounds himself with an international group which helps
him draw up a constitution for his homeland.

The group makes a number of decisions which right-
wingers would welcome. It recognizes that, if endangered,
a republic will be saved "only by people whose political persuasion is to the Right of average."[77] Even though monarchy
is rejected for Alpaca, Achala admits a "cozy feeling of regard for the British Isles and their inhabitants, with their
gentle words of veneration for Royalty."[78] The Alpaca constitution provides universal, but not uniform, suffrage. Addi-
tional votes are granted for high tax payments, scholastic
achievement, waiving of government benefits, and payment of
a poll tax. Other provisions of the constitution are also designed to reward talent. Once the document has been explained to Alpacans, all opposition melts and consequently
Juan and Mara can depend upon a happy life in a well-gov-
erned land.

Other fringe individuals and groups distributed blatant-
ly racist books. The Councilor of Shreveport, Louisiana, for
example, as late as 1973 was recommending and selling two
of Thomas Dixon's books: The Leopard's Spots (1902) and
The Clansman (1905), the book upon which The Birth of a
Nation was based.[79] In 1972, the Michigan Klan paper,
From the Mountain, published a "fable." In it King Pritchard
(President Nixon?) has surrounded himself with Rasputinger
(Kissinger?) and other "foreigners" (Jews?).[80] Earlier,
Free Men Speak (of New Orleans, and apparently related to
the efforts of Kent and Phoebe Courtney) had published The
Eagle's Feather by William Campbell Douglass, a Florida
physician who had devised "Let Freedom Ring," an "anti-
Communist telephone network." In the novel, United Nations

forces have taken over El Paso, Texas, and have made it a
neutral zone. When it announces that part of Florida will
also be taken over because of racial unrest, patriots resist.
African troops loot and rape until they meet opposition from
a handful of opponents. In disarray the black troops retreat
because they fear real violence.

NOTES

1. William A. Rusher, "Modern Morality Play," review of
    A Shade of Difference, by Allen Drury, in National
    Review, 6 November 1962, p. 357.

2. M. Stanton Evans, "The Violent Explain It Away," re-
    view of Preserve and Protect, by Allen Drury, ibid.,
    3 December 1968, p. 1225.

3. Forrest Davis, "The Age of the Shrug," review of Ad-
    vise and Consent, by Allen Drury, ibid., 29 August
    1959, p. 305.

4. Ibid.

5. Ferdinand V. Solara, Key Influences in the American
    Right (Denver: Polifax Press, 1972), p. 6.

6. Rosalie Gordon, "Great, Great, Great!" review of
    Come Nineveh, Come Tyre, by Allen Drury, in
    America's Future, 23 November 1973, p. 6.

7. Susan Ludel, "An Interview with Allen Drury," The
    Objectivist, January 1969, pp. 9-16.

8. So far nothing approaching a comprehensive biography
    of Dos Passos has appeared. Two brief books pro-
    vide overviews and basic bibliographies: George J.
    Becker, John Dos Passos, Modern Literature Mono-
    graphs (New York: Frederick Ungar Publishing Co.,
    1974) and John D. Brantley, The Fiction of John
    Dos Passos (The Hague: Mouton, 1968). For right-
    ists' statements about Dos Passos, see articles in
    National Review. Also helpful is Thomas Richard
    Gorman, "Words and Deeds: A Study of the Political

Attitudes of John Dos Passos" (Ph. D. dissertation, University of Pennsylvania, 1960).

9. Review of Sound of Thunder, by Taylor Caldwell, in National Review, 23 November 1957, p. 477.

10. Ibid.

11. Advertisement, National Review, 22 October 1960, p. 228.

12. Jess Stearn, The Search for a Soul: Taylor Caldwell's Psychic Lives (Greenwich, Conn.: Fawcett Publications, 1974).

13. Medford Evans, "Taylor Caldwell," American Opinion, October 1971, p. 35.

14. Rosalie Gordon, "Suicide of a Republic," review of A Pillar of Iron, by Taylor Caldwell, in America's Future, 12 November 1965, p. 6.

15. John W. Robbins, "Conservatism versus Objectivism," Intercollegiate Review, Winter 1969-70, p. 41.

16. Whittaker Chambers, "Big Sister Is Watching You," National Review, 28 December 1957, p. 594.

17. E. Merrill Root, "What About Ayn Rand?" ibid., 30 January 1960, pp. 76-77.

18. Garry Wills, "But Is Ayn Rand Conservative?" ibid., 27 February 1960, p. 139.

19. Letter to editor, ibid., 12 March 1960, p. 180.

20. Rosalie Gordon, "The 'Times' and 'The Fountainhead'" America's Future, 18 October 1968, pp. 5-7.

21. Root, "What About Ayn Rand?" p. 77.

22. Calumet "K", by Merwin Webster, was originally published in 1901 after it had appeared in the Saturday Evening Post. In 1967 NBI Press [Nathaniel Branden Institute, at one time an integral part of the Ayn Rand organization], published a new edition which carried an introduction by Rand. Her introduction

also appeared in The Objectivist, March 1968, pp. 7-10.

23. Human Events, 26 October 1957.

24. Medford Evans, review of Pen and Politics, by Holmes Alexander, in American Opinion, February 1970, p. 81.

25. Holmes Alexander, Pen and Politics: Autobiography of a Working Writer (Morgantown: University of West Virginia, 1970).

26. Holmes Alexander, The Equivocal Men: Tales of the Establishment (Boston: Western Islands, 1964), p. ix.

27. Ibid., p. 12.

28. Holmes Alexander, The Spirit of '76: A Political Novel of the Near Future (New Rochelle, N.Y.: Arlington House, 1966), p. 353.

29. Evans, review of Pen and Politics, p. 83.

30. W. F. Rickenbacker, review of The Equivocal Men, by Holmes Alexander, in National Review, 9 February 1965, p. 117.

31. E. M. Root, review of Shall Do No Murder, by Holmes Alexander, ibid., 15 August 1959, p. 284.

32. M. S. Evans, review of The Spirit of '76, by Holmes Alexander, ibid., 7 February 1967, p. 155.

33. Ibid.

34. F. Farr, review of West of Washington, by Holmes Alexander, ibid., 17 July 1962, p. 35.

35. Book cover.

36. Finis Farr, The Elephant Valley (New Rochelle: Arlington House, 1967), p. 122.

37. Ibid., p. 27.

38. Ibid., p. 33.

39. Ibid., p. 175.

40. P. L. Buckley, review of Elephant Valley, by Finis
    Farr, in National Review, 31 October 1967, p. 1219.

41. Rosalie Gordon, "Eye-Popping Thriller," review of Ele-
    phant Valley, by Finis Farr, in America's Future,
    22 September 1967, p. 5.

42. David O. Woodbury, Five Days to Oblivion: A Novel of
    Suspense (New York: The Devin-Adair Co., 1963),
    p. 55.

43. Ibid., p. 59.

44. Ibid., p. 78.

45. Ibid., p. 121.

46. Rosalie Gordon, "Rip-Snorting Tale," review of Five
    Days to Oblivion, by David O. Woodbury, in Amer-
    ica's Future, 21 February 1964, p. 5.

47. Ibid., p. 6.

48. Rosalie Gordon, "Excitement Aplenty," review of Mr.
    Faraday's Formula, by David O. Woodbury, in
    America's Future, 8 October 1965, pp. 5-6.

49. Ibid.

50. N. E. Adamson, Jr., review of You're Next on the
    List, by David O. Woodbury, in American Opinion,
    January 1969, pp. 87, 89, 91.

51. Victor J. Fox [pseud.], The Pentagon Case (New York:
    Freedom Press, Inc., 1958; reprinted by American
    Opinion, 1961).

52. Stephen C. Shadegg, The Remnant (New Rochelle, N.Y.:
    Arlington House, 1968), p. 332.

53. Rosalie Gordon, "Captivating, Hopeful Novel," review
    of The Remnant, by Stephen C. Shadegg, in America's
    Future, 7 June 1968, p. 6.

54. Shadegg, The Remnant, p. 19.

55. Ibid., p. 23.

56. Ibid., p. 29.

57. James H. McBride, "Handwriting on the Wall," review
     of The Journal of David Q. Little, by R. Daniel Mc-
     Michael, in Intercollegiate Review, January-March
     1968, p. 112.

58. In 1957 the same company published Ayer's account of
     his F.B.I. work, Yankee G-Man.

59. Advertisement, National Review, 16 June 1964, p. 505.

60. Ralph de Toledano, "When the Big Job Is at Stake,"
     review of The Big Man, by Henry J. Taylor, and
     Convention, by Fletcher Knebel and Charles W.
     Bailey, ibid., 4 May 1964, p. 360.

61. Ibid.

62. Jeffrey Hart, "A Rising Star," review of War Is Heav-
     en! by D. Keith Mano, ibid., 11 August 1970, p.
     847.

63. Lewis Nichols, "American Notebook," New York Times
     Book Review, 9 March 1969, pp. 18-19.

64. Hart, "A Rising Star," p. 847.

65. Ibid.

66. Tom McHale, review of The Death and Life of Harry
     Goth, by D. Keith Mano, in New York Times Book
     Review, 14 March 1971, pp. 6-7.

67. "Practicing for Death," review of The Death and Life
     of Harry Goth, by D. Keith Mano, in Newsweek, 5
     April 1971, p. 96.

68. Jeffrey Hart, " Queens Gothic," review of The Death
     and Life of Harry Goth, by D. Keith Mano, in Na-
     tional Review, 18 May 1971, pp. 543-44.

69. Reviews of The Proselytizer, by D. Keith Mano, in

Newsweek, 27 March 1972, pp. 110-11; New York
Times Book Review, 23 April 1972, pp. 4-5; and
National Review, 18 August 1972, pp. 905-06.

70. Patricia S. Coyne, "God and Mano," review of The
     Bridge, by D. Keith Mano, in National Review, 4
     January 1974, pp. 41-42.

71. Rosalie Gordon, "More Terrific 'Fiction,'" review of
     The First Team, by John Ball, in America's Future,
     10 November 1972, p. 6.

72. Rosalie Gordon, "Terrific 'Fiction,'" ibid., 13 August
     1971, p. 6.

73. Texas author file, Eugene C. Barker Library, the Uni-
     versity of Texas at Austin.

74. Revilo Oliver, review of Crossroads, by John Beaty,
     in National Review, 16 February 1957, p. 165.

75. Medford Evans, review of The Rosa Luxemburg Contra-
     ceptives Cooperative, by Leopold Tyrmand, in Amer-
     ican Opinion, December 1972, p. 87.

76. Rosalie Gordon, "Distaff David," review of An I. O. U.
     for Emily, by Lu Gene Weldon, in America's Future,
     8 December 1967, p. 5.

77. H. L. Hunt, Alpaca Revisited (Dallas: HLH Products,
     1967), p. 41.

78. Ibid., p. 42.

79. Advertisement, The Councilor, January 1973.

80. Robert E. Miles, "The Fable of Almeria," From the
     Mountain, October 1972, pp. 1-8.

CHAPTER III

OBJECTIONABLE WRITERS AND NOVELS

Equivocation is one characteristic that conservatives repudiate in liberals. Hence their own reactions to specific writers and books tend, at least on the surface, to be definitely positive or negative. And the number of books that they repudiate far surpasses the number they endorse. It must be acknowledged, though, that they are not always able to make unqualified judgments. Concerning William Faulkner, Ernest Hemingway, and even Norman Mailer, for example, they are not always at ease. Even so, a survey of their reactions to a few mainstream writers and books will demonstrate at least part of their negative literary values.

Even though conservatives recognize that "the liberals" have claimed Faulkner as one of theirs, especially because of his attitude toward blacks, some reviewers have readily admitted that the Southerner was a first-rate artist. In National Review, Robert Drake referred to him as "our greatest contemporary novelist."[1] After delineating certain internal problems of The Reivers, he praised the story's nobility and grandeur. In the same magazine, Robert Phelps described Faulkner as "the best yarn-spinner we have had since Mark Twain."[2] He believed that when Faulkner allowed himself to be drawn into travel, speech-making, and interviewing, his art had suffered. He preferred that Faulkner isolate himself and "watch what he loves, and then to write

78

about it as exactly as possible. " Phelps implied that when
the novelist attempted to "get involved," his poetic work suffered. [3] Following a similar theme, the editorial writer who
wrote Faulkner's obituary spoke warmly of the Southerner's
having created Yoknapatawpha County. The writer, though,
more heavily emphasized Faulkner's ability to withstand the
"soul-crushing assaults of the age of the masses." He also
praised Faulkner for avoiding the habits of the "Liberal Establishment" and for being "no man's and no party's fellow
traveler. "[4]

But not all responses to Faulkner were positive. In
American Opinion, Medford Evans lamented: "I should hate
to be party to a profession which has made Hemingway and
Faulkner the best known names among undergraduate students of literature. "[5] And in National Review, Garry Wills
wrote a very negative evaluation of Faulkner's work. He objected to the novelist's liberalism:

> He has no creed but compassion; he thinks in terms
> of society and its psychological patterns; his elab-
> orate and slippery form of narrative is a means of
> escaping the focus of a single person's crisis. [6]

Wills insisted that the "Snopes poison" is not to be explained
as growing out of Mississippi marshes. Faulkner, Wills believed, needed to find roots in the cleansing Yoknapatawpha
earth. Then the author could do more than merely spread
the disease of an isolated intellect. [7]

Right-wing spokesmen referred to Ernest Hemingway
as one of the "great" writers of twentieth-century America
but several aspects of his work they questioned. They appreciated him as a stylist, especially as one who tried to deal
with life without the exaggeration of romantic writers. Even

so, they usually ended on a negative note--that, while he
might have reflected a "natural piety," his refusal to acknowledge a transcendent power left his work empty. Jeffrey
Hart attempted to show that Hemingway might have been mis-
understood. Concerning A Farewell to Arms, Hart wrote
that most interpreters probably believed that the book takes
a negative view of war. Such a view, he insisted, missed
a major point of the book: the parallels between Frederic
Henry's being drawn to love Catherine Barkley and his coming to care about the war. Frederic, Hart reported, could
not "accept the pacifist simplicities of the Italian enlisted
men."[8] In short, A Farewell to Arms, according to Hart,
should not be viewed as an anti-war novel.

Hart also questioned whether or not Hemingway's religious views have been adequately understood. He suggested
that biographers have tended to pass over Hemingway's becoming a Catholic. In both National Review and Triumph,
Hart refers to A. E. Hotchner's account of Hemingway's visit
to a cathedral at Burgos, Spain. Despite injuries which resulted from a plane crash, Hemingway climbed the steps and
knelt in the sanctuary for several minutes. Hart admits that
the story does not resolve Hemingway's ultimate faith. Yet,
he concluded:

> ... it is somehow appropriate to think of Heming-
> way there in the ancient medieval cathedral in
> Burgos, for as a writer he was deeply a part of
> his civilization, and the values he celebrated, them-
> selves ancient ones, represent much that is best in
> the tradition of the West.[9]

Hemingway's obituary in National Review, though, did
not see him at the center of Western culture. The editorial
noted that great literature "is architecture whose foundations
reach down to the entrails of a culture." Hemingway's heroes,

the writer lamented, were "detached from their society, de-
racinated from the West, strangers to metaphysical reality."
More strongly, he insisted that Hemingway "didn't have the
slightest idea of what is going on in the West, of the West's
travail." Evidence: the novelist's celebration of the Republic of Spain and of Fidel Castro.[10]

No one writer evoked more negative treatment in right-
wing circles than Norman Mailer. True, conservatives sometimes admit that he has talent--even genius. William F.
Buckley, Jr. could write that "I love him as an artist ...
[because] he makes the most beautiful metaphors in the business."[11] And Joan Didion could write that: "An American
Dream is ... perhaps the only serious New York novel since
The Great Gatsby."[12] Didion praised him for his "social
eye"; Buckley found him interesting because "to many who
read him hungrily ... he represents present-day America."
But elsewhere and on other counts, right-wingers find Mailer
thoroughly objectionable.

The objections are numerous. According to John
Chamberlain, Mailer's subjects "aren't really worth his little
finger."[13] H. Kenner dismissed Deaths for the Ladies, and
Other Disasters as a foolish, embarrassing expenditure of
paper.[14] In reviewing The Armies of the Night, Jeffrey
Hart described Mailer's writing as not having "the penetration
and complexity of Batman." He also wrote that Mailer had
become a "major Talent without ever writing a good book."[15]

Some right-wing spokesmen have objected to Mailer as
a person. In American Opinion, Medford Evans admitted
that "Heretofore I have always hated Norman Mailer." He
gave three reasons for his hatred:

> (1) He is hateful, like Dr. Fell; (2) in November
> 1960 at a party in New York he stabbed his wife
> (his second one--he has had four); and, (3) he is
> a professional revolutionary. [16]

In writing up an account of Mailer's fiftieth birthday party,
D. Keith Mano reported that although talented, the alcohol-
consuming author had "herniated himself laying this egg. "[17]

Opposition to Mailer seems to boil down to two issues: his hipster style and his radical political/economic
statements. Priscilla L. Buckley pointed out that Mailer is
not really of the "have nots" with whom he persists in identifying himself. Taking such a stand, she noted, he "cannot
really understand the good square society. "[18] Likewise,
John Chamberlain objected to Mailer's making "society" an
enemy. He scoffed at Mailer's objection to conformism because: "The only 'conformism' that I see around me is the
conformism which teaches our college students that Mr.
Mailer's view of 'society' is right. "[19] Eventually, though,
the most serious objections to Mailer have to do with his
"socialistic" leanings, his stand against the war in Vietnam,
and his objections to "the military-industrial complex. "

Despite their objections, right-wing spokesmen sometimes see hope for Mailer. Buckley noted that because of
the emphasis upon the individual in Mailer's novels, the
writer is "in his own fashion, a conservative. "[20] And Medford Evans wrote that his previous hatred of Mailer had been
softened. Evans appreciated the novelist's running for mayor
of New York City on a "states' rights" platform; he also
noted some promising ethical statements in The Prisoner of
Sex that were not sacrilegious. He concluded:

> Whether or not this 'nice Jewish boy from Brooklyn'
> is likely to end up as a Louisiana-style Catholic,

it strikes a Mississippi Protestant that Norman
Mailer is looking for God.
        And since God is undoubtedly looking for
him, it well may be that they'll get together. 21

In the mid-1950s, critics in mainstream periodicals
were responding quite favorably to the work of James Gould
Cozzens.   In no uncertain terms, conservative spokesmen
reacted with scathing denunciation.   In one of the longest reviews that he has written in National Review, William F.
Buckley, Jr. attacked Cozzens' By Love Possessed.   The
only positive comment had to do with the routine acknowledgment that the author possessed talent.   Referring to several
positive statements by reviewers in mainstream circles,
Buckley begged to differ:

        ... By Love Possessed is not a good book but a
        bad one, not well written but poorly written, not
        a human document but an inhuman one. 22

He went further: "... as to whether he [Cozzens] is human,
I should say By Love Possessed leaves the question moot."
His strongest objection had to do with an implication he saw
in the book that anyone who would join the Catholic Church
is unbalanced; he suggested that Cozzens' attack resembled
the manner of the Protocols of Zion.   The reviewer claimed
not to understand why the novel of sex, iconoclasm, logorrhea,
high-class verbosity could be considered great literature.   He
wondered whether "the intellectuals" had found their Mickey
Spillane. 23
        Despite Buckley's denunciation of Cozzens' work,
seven years later Jeffrey Hart found himself defending the
novelist.   According to Hart, mainstream reviewers were now
attacking rather than praising Cozzens.   Hart concluded that
the novelist had written about "our unmentionable subject"--

social class. [24] In short, whereas Buckley had objected to
Cozzens' choice of characters, Hart was complimentary of
the author's positive treatment of the genteel rich.

Four years later when F. R. Buckley reviewed Morning Noon and Night in Triumph, he did not mention social or
political ideas but dwelt on style. Again Cozzens was treated
very negatively, but as an artist, not as philosopher or social critic. [25] In National Review, Morning Noon and Night
was reviewed by Guy Davenport, a critic whose tone and approach to books differ significantly from those of Wm. F.
Buckley and Hart. Like F. R. Buckley, Davenport pointed
out the puzzling dimensions of Cozzens' novel. Yet he found
several positive things to say of the book. Davenport's review is something of an antidote to National Review's scathing attack in 1957. [26]

Other "Establishment" writers came under criticism
in right-wing circles. Mary McCarthy was looked upon with
suspicision by John Chamberlain because of her avowed "libertarian socialism." Yet he admitted that many of her observations were conservative rather than radical. [27] E. Van
Den Haag noted that she sometimes "forays beyond her depth,"
citing her positive treatment of Hannah Arendt as an example. [28] But conservatives appreciated her ability to describe
and satirize human foibles.

Leslie Fiedler generated little positive reaction in
right-wing circles. Jeffrey Hart insisted that "after patient
searching" he (Hart) had not encountered a "wish to have
homosexual relations with Negroes and Indians."[29] Andrew
Lytle recognized some positive aspects of Love and Death in
the American Novel but questioned Fiedler's psychological
expertise. He also noted that while Fiedler claimed to con-

sider sociological, psychological, and other disciplinary techniques, he omitted references to the theological. [30] In his
review of The Last Jew in America, Guy Davenport noted
that Fiedler's characters "can never think of anything to do
but get drunk and swap insults. ... "[31]

Right-wingers castigate Saul Bellow for his adherence
to the "liberal line. " In reviewing Mr. Sammler's Planet,
John Braine explained that as a member of The Family, of
which Mary McCarthy was the matriarch, Bellow was forced
into a very rigid conformity. As Braine explained it: "a
novelist must be a heretic, he must conform to no doctrine
except that there is no doctrine. "[32] Braine objected to Bellow's treating sexual themes and suggested that "patriotism
and racialism are as strong instincts--if not stronger--than
sex. " But Bellow, he noted, following Family rules, makes
patriotism and racialism "perverted, atavistic and eventually
suicidal. "[33]

And what could one say of Portnoy's Complaint if
Sammler was too sexual? In National Review, Guy Davenport had the task of responding to Philip Roth's book. He
dealt with it in general rather than descriptive terms. He
recognized that in a free world a novelist should be free to
write as he would. But Davenport pointed out that freedom
can be abused. He also recognized that the "spirit of the
times" led writers to deal with taboo subjects in plastic
fashion. That such publications would be seen as "something
progressive" by liberals was one of Davenport's objections.
The other was that the reader would not be made "wiser or
more sensitive in understanding others. " Such a comment,
Davenport concluded, is "the saddest thing one can say of a
work of art. "[34]

F. R. Buckley was also critical of John Updike and

Gore Vidal for "wasting talent" on "tendentious dirt." Even
though Buckley acknowledged that "public taste" helped explain
"dirty books," and even though he admitted that in Couples
Updike was "expressing throughout a personal revulsion for
his times and place," he concluded with a relatively soft
statement that it was tragic that Updike felt compelled to
write as he did.   But for Vidal, he had nothing kind to say.
According to Buckley, "Bore Withal" wrote with a juvenile
pen whose "single cynical slick-sick purpose" was "to tease
money out of a public with a snout seemingly insatiably sub-
merged in the trough of genitalia."[35]   And Christopher Nichols concluded: "what Gore Vidal truly needs is for about a
million good people to intercede for him, through prayer, to
the Authority that is already there.   It just might help."[36]

      Except for books by Allen Drury and Taylor Caldwell,
popular books that made the bestseller lists, were made into movies, or were selected by large book clubs were nearly
always treated negatively by right-wing critics.   In reaction
to Hawaii, Joan Didion suggested that the book combined
travel brochure, adult daytime radio, and "A Liberal Education."   Not only did the stock characters not appeal, but the
interracial sex and "Getting-along-together" emphasis were put
in to "warm the cockles of any Liberal heart."[37]   And when
Anatomy of a Murder replaced By Love Possessed at the top
of the bestseller lists, W. F. Buckley Jr. again wrote of his
disgust that the "world of letters" was not showing any great-
er resentment than it was toward such books.   He described
Anatomy as "the worst book I can remember having read."
Yet, he noted, the author would "evidently make a fortune out
of it."   He complained that the pace was slow, the writing
execrable, plot tortured, suspense factitious, the price ex-

cessive.[38]   And Murray Kempton was equally negative about
Youngblood Hawke.   After noting that the book's "progress up
the ladder of bestsellers is as swift as its narrative is gela-
tinous," he averred that "never has a mind as trivial as
Wouk's produced a success in a style quite as tedious." He
ended with the judgment that "most of all, Wouk hates re-
finement of taste; he can function now only by believing that
Hollywood agents know better than critics."[39]

A writer in Human Events emphasized a different objection in regard to Fear of Flying by Erica Jong.   He was
incensed to learn that the author had received a $5,000 grant
from the National Endowment for the Arts.   He reported to
his readers that their tax money had been used to support a
hard-core pornographic novel.[40]

Novels that have to do with racial themes seldom get
positive receptions in right-wing periodicals.   Reviewers prefer noninflammatory stories such as Move Over Mountain by
John Ehle, a white man.[41]   Among black writers, George S.
Schuyler is one who has found himself taken in by right-wing
media.   His Black and Conservative (published by Arlington
House) and his two early novels, Black No More and Slaves
Today, represent the kind of writing by blacks that right-wing
critics can endorse.[42]   The usual response to black writers
is to acknowledge talent and then object to "propaganda."
National Review's obituary of Lorraine Hansberry suggested
that by the time of her death her impressive talent "had
boiled away in the heat of a misguided devotion to Cause."
It also noted that in her last years she had "wasted time
spitting angry clichés at pacifist meetings and race rallies."[43]

In the same magazine Andrew Lytle reviewed together
two books that concerned race: Richard Wright's The Long

Dream and Brainerd Cheney's This Is Adam. He interpreted

Cheney's treatment as a Christian one:

> Equality neither of opportunity nor of condition nor
> of intrinsic worth exists in nature nor in the arti-
> fice of the state. Order in the state depends upon
> making formal the dissimilarities and distinctions;
> only in this sense is a man free to act, because
> he is acting out of his limitations and his place.
> Any other action is license. This is the Christian
> view, which has never taken the fallen state of man
> as a happy one, nor the world as the end in it-
> self. [44]

He suggested that Wright's hatred and economic determinism

led him into "plotted" and "arbitrary" action. [45]

The content of James Baldwin's work also evoked

negative reactions. In 1962, Guy Davenport's treatment of

Another Country was gentle, for the reviewer believed that

Baldwin "neither sentimentalizes nor excuses, which is to say

that he refuses to resort either to sympathy or indifference.

He has settled for understanding alone.... "[46] But the next

year, in response to The Fire Next Time, Garry Wills took

Baldwin to task for allowing critics' objections to his neu-

trality to goad him into commitment. Wills accused the au-

thor of parading "all the liberal clichés in their pristine naiv-

eté--the wave of history, the courage to change, the need to

export our revolution. " Wills cited Baldwin's references to

" 'our curious role in Spain' and in 'pre-Castro Cuba. ' "[47]

By 1968 Davenport was criticizing Baldwin for his inflamma-

tory rhetoric and the militant implications of his novels.

Davenport seemed most put off by Baldwin's having his pro-

tagonist in Tell Me How Long the Train's Been Gone agree

to finance the arming of black power revolutionaries. [48]

Not surprisingly, conservatives take a dim view of

the work of beat writers. Robert Phelps wrote that Jack
Kerouac's Subterraneans "contains some of the most sloppy
prose ever exposed to linotype. "[49] Since Henry Miller probably did not have a conservative audience in mind when he
wrote books such as Tropic of Cancer, he would probably not
be surprised to know that a reviewer in National Review would
not respond favorably. It is unclear whether Francis Russell
is more turned off by Miller's "gallimaufry" or by Karl Sha-
piro's introduction to the Grove Press edition of Tropic of
Cancer. [50] In reaction to Lawrence Ferlinghetti's A Coney
Island of the Mind, E. Case evaluated the Beat poets:

> Although the publication of Allen Ginsberg's
> Howl gave San Francisco another famous bay, a
> title humanely sufficient for the entire donkeywork
> corpus of the San Francisco Poets might be In
> Brays of Folly. For not since the days of Dada
> has a more heavy-hoofed herd of asses jazzed the
> sacred grove of song. [51]

Another category of books which irritates right-wingers is the nuclear scare stories. Not all books which por-
tray massive destruction are objectionable to them. [52] But
books such as Nevil Shute's On the Beach are. Walter Darnell Jacobs wrote that Fail-Safe (by Eugene Burdick and Harvey Wheeler) and Seven Days in May (by Fletcher Knebel and
Charles W. Bailey II) are "political tracts designed to destroy whatever is left of American faith in the military. "[53]
Jameson G. Campaigne, Jr. rejoiced that Sidney Hook, with
the publication of The Fail-Safe Fallacy, had totally destroyed
"every serious pretension contained in the best-seller," and
had also wholly obliterated "the jungle of confusion and hys-
teria now suffocating the whole range of anti-Communist
thought and action. "[54] When Robert Goldston (The Shore

Dimly Seen) and Philip Wylie (Triumph) published novels
which also used nuclear warfare as background, William J.
Fitzpatrick was relieved that the books avoided the "dreary
catalogue of On the Beach and the specious topicality of Fail-
Safe." He also complained about the "tiresome descriptions
of vast atomic destruction" in these books. Goldston's book,
he noted, had "nothing to do with the simple-minded, paci-
fistic arguments of some of his characters." And Triumph,
he reported, "implies that America's retreats actually made
the atomic war inevitable."[55]

NOTES

1. Robert Drake, "Yoknapatawpha Innocence Lost," review
   of The Reivers, by William Faulkner, National Review, 31 July 1962, p. 72.

2. Robert Phelps, "Intruder in the Dust," ibid., 6 July
   1957, p. 43.

3. Ibid., pp. 42-43.

4. "William Faulkner, RIP," editorial, ibid., 31 July 1962,
   p. 54.

5. Medford Evans, review of Trousered Apes, by Duncan
   Williams, American Opinion, February 1973, p. 71.

6. Garry Wills, "The Thin World of the Snopeses," National
   Review, 21 November 1959, p. 498.

7. Ibid.

8. Jeffrey Hart, "War and Refuge," Triumph, April 1970,
   p. 30.

9. Ibid., p. 33.

10. "Ernest Hemingway, RIP," editorial, National Review,
    15 July 1961, p. 11.

11. William F. Buckley, Jr., "'Life' Goes to Norman Mail-

er," ibid. , 2 November 1965, p. 969.

12. Joan Didion, "A Social Eye," review of An American
    Dream, by Norman Mailer, ibid. , 20 April 1965,
    p. 329.

13. John Chamberlain, "About Us Squares," review of Ad-
    vertisements for Myself, by Norman Mailer, ibid. ,
    21 November 1959, p. 494.

14. H. Kenner, review of Deaths for the Ladies, and Other
    Disasters, by Norman Mailer, ibid. , pp. 200-201.

15. Jeffrey Hart, "Anti-matter as Jet-Set Journalism," re-
    view of The Armies of the Night, by Norman Mailer
    [and Supernation at Peace and War, by Dan Wake-
    field], ibid. , 30 July 1968, p. 754.

16. Medford Evans, review of Prisoner of Sex, by Norman
    Mailer, in American Opinion, November 1971, pp.
    81, 83.

17. D. Keith Mano, "Norman Bombs," National Review, 16
    March 1973, p. 316.

18. Priscilla L. Buckley, "Seeing It Like Mailer Does,"
    review of Miami and the Siege of Chicago, by Nor-
    man Mailer, ibid. , 11 February 1969, p. 129.

19. Chamberlain, "About Us Squares," p. 495.

20. Buckley, "'Life' Goes to Norman Mailer," p. 969.

21. Evans, review of The Prisoner of Sex, p. 91.

22. William F. Buckley, Jr. , "Gone Tomorrow," National
    Review, 26 October 1957, p. 380.

23. Ibid.

24. Jeffrey Hart, "By Ideology Possessed," ibid. , 22 Sep-
    tember 1964, p. 825.

25. F. R. Buckley, "The Crisis of Conviction," review of
    Morning Noon and Night, by James Gould Cozzens,
    in Triumph, November 1968, pp. 30-31.

26. Guy Davenport, "Parables from Inside," review of Morning Noon and Night, by James Gould Cozzens [and three other novels by different writers], in National Review, 19 November 1968, pp. 1172-73.

27. John Chamberlain, "The Conservative Miss McCarthy," ibid., 22 October 1963, pp. 353-54.

28. E. Van Den Haag, review of On the Contrary, by Mary McCarthy, ibid., 18 November 1961, p. 350.

29. Hart, "By Ideology Possessed," p. 826.

30. Andrew Lytle, "Confusion of Tongues," review of Love and Death in the American Novel, by Leslie Fiedler, ibid., 7 May 1960, pp. 301-302.

31. Guy Davenport, "Two Flops and a Winner," review of The Last Jew in America, by Leslie Fiedler [and two other books by different authors], ibid., 6 September 1966, p. 894.

32. John Braine, " Bellow's Planet," review of Mr. Sammler's Planet, by Saul Bellow, ibid., 10 March 1970, p. 264.

33. Ibid., p. 266.

34. Guy Davenport, "Cui Bono?" review of Portnoy's Complaint, by Philip Roth [and Providence Island, by Calder Willingham], ibid., 20 May 1969, p. 497.

35. F. R. Buckley, "Dirty Books: The Lay of the Land," review of Myra Breckenridge, by Gore Vidal [and other books by different authors], in Triumph, July 1968, p. 29.

36. Christopher Nichols, "Taking Up the Job God Bungled," review of Reflections upon a Sinking Ship, by Gore Vidal, in National Review, 20 May 1969, p. 499.

37. Joan Didion, "Black and White, Read All Over," review of Hawaii, by James Michener, ibid., 5 December 1959, pp. 525-26.

38. W. F. Buckley, Jr., review of Anatomy of a Murder, by Robert Traver, ibid., 11 October 1958, p. 253.

39. Murray Kempton, "The Coagulation of Herman Wouk,"
     review of Youngblood Hawke, by Herman Wouk, ibid.,
     14 August 1962, pp. 105-106.

40. John D. Lofton, Jr., "Your $5,000 Helped Bankroll
     Hard-Core Novel," Human Events, 21 June 1975, p.
     18.

41. Helen Woodward, review of Move Over, Mountain, by
     John Ehle, National Review, 22 June 1957, p. 602.

42. Schuyler has frequently written for American Opinion
     and other right-wing magazines.

43. "Lorraine Hansberry, RIP," editorial, National Review,
     26 January 1965, p. 54.

44. Andrew Lytle, "Myth or Symbol?" review of This is
     Adam, by Brainard Cheney, and The Long Dream,
     by Richard Wright, ibid., 6 December 1958, p. 375.

45. Ibid.

46. Guy Davenport, "Magic Realism in Prose," review of
     Another Country, by James Baldwin, ibid., 29 Au-
     gust 1962, p. 154.

47. Garry Wills, "What Color Is God?" review of The Fire
     Next Time, by James Baldwin, ibid., 21 May 1963,
     p. 408.

48. Guy Davenport, "If These Wings Should Fail Me, Lord!"
     review of Tell Me How Long the Train's Been Gone,
     by James Baldwin [and two other books by different
     authors], ibid., 16 July 1968, p. 701.

49. Robert Phelps, "Spring Novels," review of The Sub-
     terraneans, by Jack Kerouac [and other books by
     different authors], ibid., 19 April 1958, p. 377-78.

50. Francis Russell, "The Cult of Henry Miller," review of
     Tropic of Cancer, by Henry Miller, ibid., 12 August
     1961, pp. 92-94.

51. E. Case, review of A Coney Island of the Mind, ibid.,
     6 December 1958, p. 380.

52. Alas Babylon, by Pat Frank, and If All the Rebels Die,
     by Samuel B. Southwell met with their approval.
     National Review, 26 September 1959, p. 371, and 9
     August 1966, p. 796.

53. Walter Darnell Jacobs, "Home-Made Holocaust," re-
     view of Fail-Safe, by Eugene Burdick and Harvey
     Wheeler, and Seven Days in May, by Fletcher Knebel
     and Charles W. Bailey II, ibid., 4 December 1962,
     pp. 444-45.

54. Jameson G. Campaigne, Jr., "On Target," review of
     The Fail-Safe Fallacy, by Sidney Hook, ibid., 19
     November 1963, p. 444.

55. William J. Fitzpatrick, "You Can Wait for the Movie,"
     review of The Shore Dimly Seen, by Robert Goldston,
     and Triumph, by Philip Wylie, ibid., 7 May 1963,
     pp. 372-73.

CHAPTER IV

RECURRING THEMES IN RIGHT-WING
NOVELS AND CRITICISM

What qualities do right-wing reviewers demand of a
book? In the most popular magazines, they prefer books
that are exciting, yet realistic; frightening, yet encouraging.
In America's Future, Rosalie Gordon praised The First Team
because it was "hopeful, inspiring, a story to recapture once
more pride and patriotism in the hearts of Americans."[1]
One finds a reviewer forgiving the "failures of style and
novelistic accoutrements" because a book reaches "down to
the gut of the people."[2] While there are varying criticisms
and even tolerances on certain points, one demand is always
constant: that writers not employ "Freudo-Marxist" principles to interpret the American tradition. In contrast, a
"Christian appraisal" will likely receive a positive response.[3]
      One way to understand rightists' expectations of fiction
is to examine the kind of character that they expect a protagonist to be. In contrast to mainstream writers, whom
Stephen Tonsor accused of favoring characters "so small that
even their sins become improbable,"[4] right-wing authors focus upon characters of heroic proportions. Throughout The
Spirit of '76, President Jeremiah Chase is described as a
modern-day George Washington, whose integrity and political
sagacity are mythical in dimension. And in Crossroads,
John Beaty glorifies the Southern gentlemanly qualities of the
central character, a person seemingly incapable of even being

tempted to err, much less partake of evil doings. In The
Devil's Advocate and The Journal of David Q. Little, the authors choose as saviors of the nation men who, until exigencies call forth their superhuman integrity and strength,
have been rather ordinary businessmen. As presented by the
authors, the men turn out to be among the very few elites to
be found in millions; others are hopeless compromisers.
And the idea of a saving remnant, a precious few who have
not "bowed their knees to Baal," is developed in Shadegg's
The Remnant. The author, who is an avid Goldwater sup-
porter, obviously gave his fictional hero the virtues he sees
in the Arizona Senator. The character is also fashioned in
the likeness of an Old Testament prophet.

     Sexual lapses among right-wing protagonists result
from different causes than among other men. Some acts,
of course, are outside the pale. In Advise and Consent,
Senator Brig Anderson, though a sympathetic character, is
not allowed to escape penalty for his loneliness-inspired,
youthful involvement with a fellow male on an isolated military post. So he pays for his indiscretion with an honorable
suicide. In some cases, adultery is not a sign of weakness,
but of admirable virility. David Q. Little becomes sexually
involved with a friend's wife who, like himself, is married
to a spouse who refuses to oppose the political decay that is
rapidly engulfing the nation. Senator Fessenden of The Remnant also finds temporary solace with a Mexican-American
woman when his eastern, aristocratic wife is unable to maintain her vitality amidst the political chaos which grows out
of her husband's unbending righteousness. And premarital
sex is not always viewed negatively, for another right-wing
protagonist, Philip Obermeister, an unmarried man who appears in two of Holmes Alexander's books, is not considered

unethical when he turns to temporary bed partners after one
of the women he admires refuses to abandon her fidelity to
her husband who has fled to the U. S. S. R. and another refuses to abandon her membership in a chastity club.

But often right-wing protagonists are puritanical in
their sexual conduct. In The Spirit of '76 President Chase
is married to a neurotic woman, but he remains faithful to
her, seemingly able to eschew any temptation to turn to other
women. And in Crossroads the central character is so upright that he repudiates his virginal childhood sweetheart after
he discovers her dancing in a local roadhouse.

Except in rare circumstances, such as warfare, sympathetic characters in right-wing novels are honest; often
they seem to enjoy being undiplomatically blunt. Even politicians are committed to speaking unequivocably, regardless
of the consequences. For example, Senator Fessenden of
The Remnant stands by his word, even when the President
asks him to reconsider an announcement that the Senator
would not seek reelection. Prefacing his act of rebellion
against his party leaders with a disclaimer that he is acting
for political reasons, demonstrating his sincerity, he dramatically repudiates continuance in the august office. When
results of his action convince the party leaders that the Senator is correct, they capitulate, offering him an even more
honorable place in the party than he has had. But nothing
doing. At the end of the book, the honest man stands by
his word. In America's Future, Rosalie Gordon reports that
The Ass that Went to Washington "will enthrall those who
still believe that words mean what they say."[5]

But in circumstances where it is appropriate, right-
wing characters become masters of deception. In The Devil's
Advocate, the Minute Men construct a nationwide organization

which is highly efficient. Even though the system requires
complex orchestration, none of the essential secrets is exposed. And such resourcefulness is not limited to the art of
deceiving. Seldom do right-wing protagonists make mistakes
in judgment; their political acumen is at times grandiose.
Within hours of taking office, President Chase in The Spirit
of '76 neutralizes a pushy wife of the deceased President who
over the years has built a popularly received plan to make
her son president. In a very simple maneuver, Chase over-
turns her years of efforts and redirects the mass support to
himself rather than to the charismatic young man who is obviously meant to resemble one of the Kennedy brothers. The
protagonist of The Devil's Advocate knows how, instantaneous-
ly, to subvert a system which has been developing for years.
The army, supported by privileged, wealthy farmers, runs
the country. Its power seems absolute. Yet the protagonist
is able to alienate the farmers, motivate the masses to refuse to respond to psychological manipulation, and soon return the country to its former ways. And with few casual-
ties. Such achievements are not brought about by ordinary
mortals, but by supermen.

　　　　To be a right-wing hero or heroine, a character must
be a person of action. To win, one must attack, not merely
defend. [6] Neutralism on any issue is unthinkable; equivocation is a liberal disease. According to Holmes Alexander,
equivocation is the fatal flaw which explains why worthy men
allowed the nation to decline from a position of supremacy
to one of parity. [7] He admits that he is building upon Allen
Drury's reference in Advise and Consent to the "chief villain ... 'the most dangerous man in America--the Equivocal
Man.'"[8] A wait-and-see or laissez-faire attitude toward
evil is looked upon as sheer folly. Right-wing readers re-

spond enthusiastically to Quixotic figures such as the heroine
of An I.O.U. for Emily, who ingeniously takes on the entire
federal government (including the Army) because she can no
longer endure participating in the Social Security program.
Although the government does not fall, it is brought into "de-
licious turmoil" by a single individual. The reviewer in
America's Future admits that it is just a story; one that will
appear dangerous to retreaters, but "to male and female
Davids most inviting."[9]

But right-wing protagonists can be arrogantly ingeni-
ous and authoritatively active only under limited circumstances.
It is acceptable for them to attack evil, but in ordinary times
they must be humble, even self-effacing. The quiet, peace-
loving man or woman--satisfied to live in a great land, often
in a pastoral setting, not the assertive, verbal, driven ac-
tivist who wants a better world--is the stereotype American
that right-wingers admire. Robert Phelps likes Holger Cahill's The Shadow of My Hand, which describes Dakota farmers whom, Phelps suggests, city slickers would call "hicks."[10]
In The Spirit of '76 President Chase acts in an almost de-
monic fury to settle foreign and domestic problems--then he
graciously repudiates presidential power so that he can re-
tire to a quiet Virginia farm to be a peaceful, country gentleman. His greatness seems to lie in his uncanny way of knowing when to be aggressive and when to be retiring.

Such an ability to make proper judgments grows out
of a character's "instinctive morality." In essence, the pos-
session of such virtue is evidenced by a protagonist's ability to recognize the modern, universal collectivist conspiracy
in whatever form it might appear. Rightists attribute to
mainstream writers an inability to perceive a fundamentally
evil nature of communism. In their eyes, moderates and

leftists not only fail to recognize danger, but also lack a suf-
ficiently positive appreciation for the American system. Moderates supposedly lack a "stirring certainty" about religious
faith or constitutional principles--two phrases which come
close to being treated as synonyms. The absence of "passionate belief" results in the characters created by liberals
being equivocal and nonaggressive at critical moments.

Another way to approach right-wing attitudes toward
characters is to look at what critics in rightist sources have
to say about fiction written by liberals. In the National Review, Robert Phelps objected to Truman Capote's Breakfast
at Tiffany's because the heroine comes from "society's maverick margin."[11] In Image of Life, John Beaty accuses
modern writers of sitting down beside a cesspool and stirring
it. He objects to the treatment--positive or negative--of that
"small segment of the population that curses every age," that
minority which "should be of concern to the lawmakers, jail-
ers, and executioners" but which should not receive the attention of artists.[12] The existential antihero has no champions among right-wing spokesmen. Thus Duncan Williams'
interpretation of such characters as "trousered apes" found
a ready acceptance by right-wing critics.[13]

In addition to right-wingers' notions about what protagonists should be, there are other expectations that set
them apart from mainstream thinkers. One issue concerns
loyalty. Because the republic, according to Forrest Davis
in National Review, is "immemorially worthy of high devotion,"[14] right-wing spokesmen expect--rather, demand--that
there never be any doubt about a book's ultimate tone: it
must be unambiguously patriotic. They cannot understand
why any author would waver in making clear where allegiance
belongs. Such unwavering commitment is made clear by the

central character of H. L. Hunt's Alpaca when he says: "I
love my country more than life itself. "[15] In American Opinion, E. Merrill Root wrote that patriotism demands reverence for the nation, a reverence stemming from a "mystical
union and communion with the land and the spirit of the land,
with the people and the spirit of the people. "[16] In the same
article he noted how refreshing it is "amid our contemporary
anvil chorus celebrating what is wrong with America, to hear
a clear and powerful voice proclaiming what is right with
America. "[17] He describes Kenneth Roberts' books as ones
that "can grow only out of a love that throbs in the red ar-
terial substance of the heart. "[18]

    Even so, most right-wing fiction is not positive in
tone.   The negative emphasis, however, must be used against
disloyal Americans.   As a matter of fact, and even though
they would likely not welcome the notion, right-wing critics
and writers dwell far more noticeably on negative rather than
positive themes.   They glory in stories which emphasize not
why and how Americans could or might lose their freedom
and well-being but why and how they are losing them.   Nega-
tivism and urgent pleas for change must always be in the interest of returning the country to a previous stage, never
for disestablishing or drastically modifying traditional institutions.

    Feeling as deeply as they do about the country, right-
wingers cannot endure political irreverence--especially on the
part of liberals.   Even they admit that an absence of a sense
of humor marks their ranks.   And chief among the culprits
they despise is the creator of the Herblock cartoons.   John
Chamberlain objected to the cartoons because a "fathomless
stupidity directs an admittedly competent draughtsmanship. "[19]
And William S. Schlamm could see no reason "why ten million

people should pay attention to Mr. Block's political findings which, to tell the truth, are not only wrong but stupid. "[20] He contended that Herblock follows the "orthodox party line of Americans for Democratic Action, a notoriously artless political cabal. "[21]   But satire, of course, can be employed against the enemies of the nation.   Right-wingers welcomed Al Capp to their corner, obviously hoping that they would have a counterpart of Herblock.   But as Capp's popularity dwindled in proportion to the growth of his enthusiasm for right-wing causes, one of his new-found allies, William F. Buckley, Jr. , claimed "conspiracy. "[22]   And Buckley described a similar drop in the popularity of Mort Sahl when the comedian dared criticize John F. Kennedy in the same way that he had ridiculed President Eisenhower. [23]

In place of irreverence, right-wing critics would have books that positively treat what they consider the glorious dimensions of the American experience.   For example, they always react favorably to books that endorse the agrarian myth.   According to E. Merrill Root, patriotism is rooted in the soil.   Hence he praised Kenneth Roberts' Northwest Passage because it portrays "landscapes of patriotism" which moderns, "whose roots have been torn up, who have been eliminated from the soil that nourishes the soul, " do not know. [24]   Other critics praise accounts of men and women "on the earth" living "cleanly unbureaucratized lives. "[25]

Right-wing spokesmen welcome books that glorify the Golden Age of America and books that lament its passing. The line of demarcation is generally the election of Franklin D. Roosevelt in 1932.   Prior to that time, American giants supposedly had achieved great things.   In The Remnant, [26] one of the characters praises those who "reached for the stars, " who "beat out their own destiny, " who conquered the wilder-

ness, who made the land a "haven of refuge for the weary
and the oppressed," and who created opportunities for the
ambitious. [27] But unfortunately, as right-wing spokesmen see
recent history, the golden age dimmed.   Medford Evans lamented the passing of "the brave (as it used to be) New
World. "[28] And in the introduction to Calumet K, Ayn Rand
suggested that the subtitle of the book should be This Was
America. [29] In The Devil's Advocate, Taylor Caldwell describes the sacrifice (from the early thirties) of freedom,
pride, responsibility, grandeur, and strength by the "loath-
some use of the word 'security. '"[30] Before that time, "there
was no body of people who believed themselves to be 'common men' or underprivileged. "[31]

More strongly than they react favorably to patriotic
war novels, right-wing reviewers react negatively to anti-
military stories.   In National Review, Walter Darnell Jacobs
concluded that there is probably not a conspiracy behind the
appearance of such books as Fail Safe and Seven Days in
May, but he indicted the authors for being heretical and
"criminally" absurd.   Just what made them criminal was not
made clear. [32] Rosalie Gordon welcomed William Chamberlain's Red January as an antidote to the "spate of leftish scare
novels and movies" which she described as "specious, highly
inaccurate but dramatic attempts at making us think, whether
the authors so intended it or not, that it's better to be Red
than dead. "[33] And again in the National Review, William J.
Fitzpatrick complained about the "tiresome descriptions of
vast atomic destruction. " Rather than shelters from bombs,
he recommended shelters against "the fall-out of gimmick literature which rains down on us. "[34] Whatever the danger,
according to President Chase in The Spirit of '76, "it's almost
better to go ahead and have a nuclear war than be afraid of it. "[35]

Another recurring strain in right-wing fiction has to
do with American nativism. Anti-Catholicism, a major nativistic theme in the nineteenth and early twentieth centuries,
is not apparent. As a matter of fact, the Buckley family
publications and other similar ones represent frankly and
strongly the Catholic traditions. But other elements of nativism are apparent. The positive treatment of the Anglo-
Saxon tradition is not always blatant, but it is frequently sub-
sumed into such wording as "Western," "Christian," "previous structures," "natural distinctions," and "the old order."
Richard M. Weaver, a frequent contributor to National Review and other conservative journals, wrote that "one does
not have to be either Anglo-Saxon or Anglo-phile to be an
American," but, according to him, "one does have to accept
certain principles."[36] John Beaty's Crossroads, which was
highly recommended by Revilo Oliver in National Review, pre-
sents a modern-day statement of the Old South mythologies.

On the negative side there are three basic nativistic
emphases in right-wing fiction. Anti-immigration sentiment
received what may be its bluntest statement in H. L. Hunt's
Alpaca Revisited. In it, one of the characters points out
that political revolutions "are the bitter fruit of unrestricted
immigration and carelessly administered immigration laws."[37]
Other treatments were less blunt. In The Spirit of '76, a
Puerto Rican immigrant who is a military pilot assassinates
a popular American president in an effort to call attention to
the Puerto Rican cause. Villains in other right-wing novels
are frequently immigrants.

Anti-Semitism is also apparent in some right-wing
criticism. In reviewing Podhoretz' Making It, Jeffrey Hart
complained that the "American Literary Establishment" is
really a Jewish "family." But he qualified his idea by point-

ing out that it is politics, rather than Judaism per se, that
provides group identity. Hence non-Jews such as Mary Mc-
Carthy and Dwight MacDonald could be assimilated into the
family.[38]   And Robert O. Bowen regaled Robert Penn Warren
for playing up Southern anti-Semitism in Wilderness. Bowen
concluded that "Chauvinism is bad enough for members of the
family, but Warren's excesses find no apology."[39]

    In spite of their insistence that liberals dodge sticky
issues by doubletalking and blurring meanings, right-wing authors and critics seldom speak unequivocably regarding American racial issues.   They may well admit that citizens deserve rights and also that Afro-Americans have been blatantly
discriminated against.   But then they tend to qualify their
statements.   Black persons frequently are villains in right-
wing novels.   In Eagle's Feather, black United Nations troops
are pictured as bloodthirsty rapists who also are cowards.
In reviewing Hawaii, Joan Didion castigated James Michener
for involving white women sexually with Kelly, a dark Hawaii-
an of Oriental ancestry.[40]   And in A Shade of Difference,
Allen Drury frequently refers to cannibalism and other un-
civilized customs of new African nations which, by inference,
the author believes should have no major voice in the United
Nations.   Regarding American blacks, Holmes Alexander has
a black character in The Spirit of '76 think to himself:

> Most everywhere, he had to admit, Negroes were
> the hoodlums of the street, the breeders of vast
> numbers of illegitimate babies, the soakers-up of
> relief and special-favor money which came largely
> from white pockets.   The American majority was
> willing to forget all this group delinquency whenever
> a Negro individual made good.... It was true in
> his own case.   It could be true for all Negroes....[41]

    In less stark ways, right-wing writers tend to accept

the traditional southern white attitude toward blacks. In such
an approach certain themes emerge: 1) Blacks are different, and the nation would be unwise to try to ignore "natural
distinctions"; 2) Integration will occur only slowly; efforts to
speed it up will likely slow it down; 3) Even in the absence
of tensions, miscegenation is objectionable[42]; 4) There has
been a misunderstanding of the Southern tradition; 5) Brutal
treatment of blacks in the South has been greatly overempha-
sized by the outside press; 6) Blacks really do not want integration. Almost without exception, the civil rights movement is interpreted by right-wingers as a subversive movement manipulated by foreigners. They blame communists for
most of the racial troubles in the United States.

There are a number of other ways in which right-
wingers reflect their attitudes toward race issues. House
servants are nearly always black or Oriental. Positively
treated in right-wing novels are gentle, rational, patient
blacks who work within the system. And the negative criticism far outweighs the positive in right-wing periodicals regarding books by black novelists and poets--usually intense
people who are not acquiescent in tone.

As strongly as they react negatively to racially-ori-
ented themes, right-wing critics welcome positive treatments
of American capitalism--preferably as it existed before the
1930s. They see no value in books which debunk the system.
Yet, as John Chamberlain pointed out in National Review, no
one has yet demonstrated whether "business as business" is
subject matter for "truly great fiction."[43] It is in this area,
though, that right-wingers can appreciate Ayn Rand. They
also praise John Dos Passos for his apparent change of attitude toward the economic system in his later years.

In conjunction with their praise for the American eco-

nomic system, right-wingers oppose benevolence. In The
Remnant, Senator Fessenden opposes the "whole apparatus of
benevolent big brother"; he objects to those who seem "unable to escape a sense of guilt over the success of America. "[44] On another occasion in the same book, another character proposes that one can give to others "friendship, understanding, encouragement, sympathy and new knowledge. " But,
he avers, "No man has the right to give things of great material value to another man unless the gift is earned. "[45]

In right-wing novels, then, charitable organizations
are always treated negatively. In Alpaca Revisited one of
Hunt's characters reports that "charities frequently fall into
the hands of the enemies of Freedom. "[46] Right-wing critics
fail to appreciate the role of such organizations whether they
be involved in direct material relief programs or in more
abstract crusades--such as Holmes Alexander's "Lobby for a
Loveable World" in The Spirit of '76. [47] Rather than seeing
humanitarian organizations as being primarily the response to
needs which are not being adequately met by existing institutions, right-wingers see them as counter-agencies designed
to criticize if not to destroy existing economic and political
institutions. Men, it would appear, should depend upon their
resources, rather than looking to eleemosynary organizations.

Opposition to socialized medicine, a major theme in
right-wing thinking, is usually a minor theme in fiction.
There apparently has been no novel so far which focuses
primarily upon the dark consequences of public medicine.
But on the extreme right, The Eagle's Feather (written by a medical doctor) focuses upon a patriotic doctor who opposes collectivistic trends domestically and internationally. In less
radical circles, the theme of socialized medicine is usually
treated as a minor part of a story. In Holmes Alexander's

West of Washington, for example, there is a passing reference to a couple's going to a fertility clinic because they have
been unable to have children. The female counselor, a blunt,
gruff person, speaks so directly that the husband is humili-
ated. A reader could well read the section without noting
that the tone of the doctor has anything to do with the service being sponsored by a public agency. Yet Finis Farr in
the National Review reported that the incident is an appalling
picture of what lies ahead when the federal government takes
over the practice of medicine. [48]

Allen Drury is able to combine internationalism and
socialized medicine. In A Shade of Difference, the United
Nations doctor is pictured as an "owlish" person who is in-
competent and who apparently has the job as a political sine-
cure. And in Taylor Caldwell's futuristic dystopia, one of
the characters muses about what happened to the medical
profession:

> Durant remembered what his father and older
> friends had once told him of the ancient and honor-
> able profession of medicine. There had been a
> time when physicians had been men of independence,
> pride and stature. They had reached their present
> level of degradation not so much by pressure of
> governmental totalitarian agencies as by their own
> lack of self-respect and courage, their own unwill-
> ingness to fight for the liberty of their profession.
> True, there had been hundreds of incompetents
> among them, twenty or thirty years ago, who could
> not make a living in free competition, and who had
> been eager to surrender their freedom for a na-
> tionalized salary. But these had been a minority.
> It was the cynicism, the absence of character and
> resolution among the majority of the profession
> which had reduced it to a slave service. [49]

Social Security is another benevolent program that in-
furiates right-wingers. It is never interpreted as an insur-

ance policy but as an imposition which costs far more than
it pays.   More irritating is the fact that it is a federal project; were it local or state-supported, supposedly it would be
less objectionable.   The symbolic implications of a nine-digit
number assigned to each person would seem to be the most
easily exploited facet of the system.   One of the major ways
that the central character of An I. O. U. for Emily is able to
persuade all the people of her town to rebel against paying
taxes is to remind them of their "dehumanization" through the
assigned social security number.

It is especially galling to right-wingers that Americans
do not actively oppose unwelcomed developments such as the
Social Security program and other "collectivistic" trends.   According to them, to be noncommunist is not enough--one must
be anticommunist.   The world, as they see it, is divided into two camps.   They abhor the notion that "communists are
just like all other civilized beings. "[50]   The definition of a
communist--"Never mind the dictionary or legalistic definition"[51]--is:

> But to be a communist could be to adhere to the
> party without belonging to it, to support its fronts
> with contributions and to back its political purposes
> with influence as well as money.   To be a com-
> munist might be so liberal as to be a leftist, and
> so much a leftist as to be in favor of making Amer-
> ica over into a socialist state with pacifist tenden-
> cies. [52]

Right-wingers denounce cooperation with "Reds" because it
will inevitably lead to a "downgrading of national defenses. "[53]
"If there are Communists in it, it's a Communist movement....   If they're not in command right now, they will be
later. "[54]

Right-wingers will not admit that any aspect of Russian

life can be positive.   To meet their approval any book on the
subject must depict the Soviet system as the antithesis of the
American.   William Rusher objected to Mitchell Wilson's
treatment of Stalinism and McCarthyism as two similar hide-
ous styles. [55]   In The Remnant, as well as other novels, the
Russian people are pictured as not really wanting or supporting communism. [56]   What is true for the U. S. S. R. applies to
other Marxist states as well, especially China.

Right-wing reviewers look askance at any leveling notions of liberal and radical writers.   As they view history,
"the few always have had and always will have a good chance
of cozening their brethren, and will take it, education be
hanged. "[57]   Richard M. Weaver accused Harvey Wish of
"pleading for a kind of featureless social order which histor-
ically is not ours. "[58]   Jeffrey Hart complained that "Social
class is our unmentionable subject. "[59]   In American Opinion,
Medford Evans endorsed Duncan Williams' observation that
there is a connection between equalitarianism and degener-
acy. [60]   And in Alpaca Revisited, H. L. Hunt would substitute
for uniform suffrage a graduated system which recognizes
that some persons contribute more than others. [61]

There are other implications of elitism in right-wing
thinking.   There seem to be two bases for setting some persons apart from others--one is inherited, superior talent.
In The Devil's Advocate, one of Taylor Caldwell's characters
notes that "still the superior are born, here and there.   Not
very many, and in diminishing quantities. "[62]   Along these
lines, Ayn Rand's ideas merge with right-wing thinking.   She
looks longingly back to the nineteenth century as a "world in
which ability mattered. "[63]   But there is a second characteristic reflected by right-wing elitists, a moral superiority.
Several writers emphasize that the nation, if it is to be saved,

will survive because of the presence of a few upright patriots. In The Remnant, one man's integrity is enough to turn about the political drift of the entire leadership of the federal government.   In The Devil's Advocate, Minute Men are described as a "few sane souls in one vast prison of madmen."[64]   Wealth, of course, is looked upon as one of the most dependable indications that a man is both talented and virtuous.   Hence it is very painful for one of the characters in The Spirit of '76 to have to lament that "we're now forced to treat poor people better than rich people."[65]

Right-wing critics accept with relish fictional accounts of communists and fellow travelers who leave the cause after becoming disillusioned.   Although such confessions comprise a major part of right-wing book offerings, few of them are presented as novels.   Their main selling point is that they are realistic.   But there are exceptions.   Grace Lumpkin's Full Circle, a thinly veiled fictional treatment of the involvement in and withdrawal from the American Communist Party by the author and her daughter, is one of the few "fictional" treatments.

Since so much right-wing ideology rests upon opposition to the Marxist systems in the U.S.S.R., China, and other nations, right-wing spokesmen take a keen interest in American diplomacy.   Besides the touchstone of opposing communism around the globe, several other themes appear in right-wing fiction concerning diplomacy.   The long-standing opposition to taxing American citizens so that money can be "given" to other countries through programs such as the Marshall Plan is one such theme.[66]   Another is the scornful repudiation of "peace-at-any-pricers, the unilateral disarmers, the cooperators-with-communism."[67]   Collective security receives a resounding debunking in favor of bilateral poli-

cies[68] enforced by a president who does not believe that
there is "something sinful in the frank use of force to imple-
ment" the nation's commitment to such policies.[69] "Coex-
istence" is seen as being synonymous with "collectivism and
surrender."[70]

Collectivism in diplomacy, of course, is the essence
of the United Nations ideal, and understandably right-wingers
are vehement in their denunciation of that organization. Often
the criticism is left in very general terms, as in William A.
Rusher's comment in the National Review, that the United Nations is "doing deadly and increasing damage to the cause of
freedom everywhere."[71] Other criticisms have to do with
third world nations. In Alpaca Revisited, the author laments:
"A tiny nation, even though it be composed of ignorant sav-
ages and cannibals incapable of governing themselves, has
equal vote with all other UN members."[72] Allen Drury's A
Shade of Difference paints an equally bleak picture of the
primitive status of some United Nations members. But ultimately opposition rests upon the supposition that the U.S.S.R.
controls the United Nations. In the Journal of David Q. Little it is put in blunt terms: "The Soviet Empire is the World
Order of Nations, and the whole world is the Soviet Empire."[73] "World opinion" is seen as a myth that requires
"no apology and certainly no obeisance."[74]

While anticommunism is undoubtedly the most obvious
common element of various right-wing camps, opposition to
the federal government is another frequent emphasis. Somehow the national government takes on an evil nature which
state and local governments do not. But ultimately it is
clear that the opposition is based upon the social programs
of the government--integration, welfare, medical care, education, and other such endeavors--rather than upon some well-

defined ideological tenet.   The power of the federal government to levy an income tax undoubtedly provides a major, if
not the most significant, basis for criticism.

But then, it would seem that the opposition to a strong
government stems from its commitments rather than its power.   If the government were committed to acceptable econom-
ic/social policies, it would undoubtedly have right-wing support.   In several novels, for example, there is criticism of
Congress for reducing military expenditures.   Nowhere is
there a suggestion that a strong standing army is possible
without a strong national government.   There is a noticeable
strain of appreciation for authoritarian efficiency in a number of right-wing novels.   Strong men whose ultimate commitment is to freedom assume power and in a heavy-handed
way set institutions aright, then step down.

The Supreme Court also comes under bitter criticism
in right-wing fiction.   Critics have some problems here because they see that until recent decades the court was the
most conservative branch of government.   Therefore, the
right-wing cannot repudiate the court but instead argues that
it should return to its previous values.   In other words, the
court has been subverted.   In The Remnant, the author has
one of the characters wondering how much the Warren Court
decisions were "the working of the Court, how much a re-
flection of the tolerance and surrender injected into the life-
blood of the Republic like a deadly virus by the liberal here-
sies."[75]   Although the statement is difficult to decipher, it
represents both the abstract nature of right-wing arguments
against the court and the difficulty in upholding the right of
the court to interpret the law while denying it the right to be
influenced by historical developments.   In Allen Drury's novels, the author pictures one of the judges as being a "flaming

liberal" who actively participates in a number of shady political shenanigans.

Without exception, in right-wing fiction mass protests
against the United States Government are always described as
being controlled by communists. Conservatives can accept
the right to criticize the American system if the critics first
unequivocably affirm their faith in the system. A mass protest would apparently be acceptable if it were clear that the
participants loved the country and wanted to return it to a
previous status. The malcontents who will not affirm their
loyalty and who want to change the system to a more non-
traditional one are the inexcusable ones. And right-wing
novels frequently focus upon violence done to innocent persons
as a result of mob protests. In The Spirit of '76, a mob in-
timidates the wife of the president in a way which recalls the
treatment of Mrs. Andrew Jackson. In Capable of Honor,
the pregnant daughter-in-law of the Secretary of State is phys-
ically assaulted by a mob.

Right-wing critics welcome and endorse futuristic novels which apply Orwell's 1984 theme to the American situation. The Journal of David Q. Little, by R. Daniel Mc-
Michael, was praised as such a book. [76] Taylor Caldwell's
The Devil's Advocate is probably the best-known and most appreciated of the genre in right-wing circles. And on this
point, Ayn Rand's Atlas Shrugged squares well with right-
wing attitudes that growing benevolent sentiment and the par-
allel development of paternalistic government will result in
the destruction of the American society.

Right-wing spokesmen emphasize individualism as a
major tenet of their ideology. From the negative angle,
Theodore Sturgeon set forth his view of human potential by
advocating intolerance of the posture which implies that "man's

acts and man's inspiration are incapable, unassisted, of solving man's problems. "[77] Positively, a reviewer of Finis Farr's The Elephant Valley praised the book for demonstrating what a single individual can accomplish despite "obfuscation, confusion, and outright conspiracy. "[78] In The Devil's Advocate, one explanation for the collapse of the American system is that too many persons had been anxious to believe that the government "would solve problems for them which had been pridefully solved, many times over, by their fathers. "[79] Ayn Rand resurrected Calumet "K", a story originally published early in the century, because it "has one element that I have never found in any other novel: the portrait of an efficacious man. "[80] The story glorifies a man's ingenuity "in solving unexpected problems and smashing through sudden obstacles, his self-confident resourcefulness, his inexhaustible energy, his dedication. " Such a person "takes nothing for granted, " "thinks long-range, " and "assumes responsibility as a matter of course, as a way of life, knowing that there is no such thing as 'luck. '"[81]

Other novels emphasize similar themes. In reviewing Kenneth Roberts' Boon Island, E. M. Root pointed out that "it affirms the fundamental stark courage of the human heart, the persistence of the human will to endure the unendurable. "[82] In The Remnant, the protagonist believes that no one wants "to do anything for himself anymore. "[83] Later the same speaker asserts:

> If the illiterate, the uneducated, could be inspired to thirst for knowledge, they would find a way to satisfy that aspiration. If the poor and the dispossessed would only concentrate their creative efforts on escaping from their miserable environment, the opportunities of America would be their pathway to a more abundant life. [84]

A reading of right-wing fiction reveals that its advocates have a surface skepticism toward "intellectuals." They
assign major significance to what liberal writers and teachers
say. For example, in American Opinion, Medford Evans
claimed that in the place of declining clerical influence,
teachers of English literature are probably the "most influen-
tial class of people in America--influential regarding personal
life style and philosophic orientation."[85] Yet they insist that
the common man is better able than intellectuals to understand issues and cope with the issues the nation faces. In
The Spirit of '76, a diplomat who is able to put the Russians
in their place is described as an "undistinguished, overweight,
bureaucratic hack" who does not "go into a flap the way the
top-level intellectuals did."[86] In Alpaca, the group which
draws up a new constitution decides that many "of the bad
political decisions which have blackened human history have
been made by so-called 'educated' people whose minds have
been warped and twisted by bookish theories which have no
relationship to political reality."[87] Yet in Alpaca, the "educated" are to be given more votes than the uneducated. And
it is quite apparent that right-wing spokesmen want to be ac-
corded respectability as intellectuals. In its absence they
react in understandable bitterness. Hence in National Review,
Anthony Lejeune can dismiss as "high brow critics ... and
amateur sociologists" those who accuse Ian Fleming of ex-
ploiting sex and sadism.[88]

Among "intellectuals," right-wingers hold psychologists
and psychiatrists in utmost contempt. In The Elephant Valley one of the characters agrees with the protagonist that
"most of these people [psychiatrists] are half cracked, undoubtedly." But, the man concludes, "they have power."[89]
In the novel, Dr. Greenway, who on the basis of a two-min-

ute interview concludes that the protagonist has latent trans-
vestite tendencies, gets the central character cashiered out
of the fictional C.I.A.   And in The Devil's Advocate, Taylor
Caldwell explains:

> Durant was well acquainted with psychia-
> trists. He knew their twentieth century history,
> their jargon, and the powerful position they occu-
> pied in The Democracy. They, more than any oth-
> er single group, had been instrumental in promot-
> ing the awful degradation of the human spirit not
> only in America but in all other nations. [90]

There is no uniform agreement in right-wing circles
about religion.   For some individuals and groups, religion
is the basic tie.   Others repudiate belief in the supernatural.
The atheistic element of Ayn Rand's ideas is the one which
sets her apart from right-wingers in general.   In a way,
her emphasis upon the individual pushes her away from the
need for the spiritual.   But in the theistic circles, there is
a strong emphasis upon the need for an individual to be sub-
missive to the supernatural.   In both Protestant and Catholic
groups there is a common emphasis upon a transcendent power, yet apparently there has been no attempt to analyze the
effects of the two contrasting attitudes--priesthood of the individual and the infallibility of the hierarchy--on social thinking among right-wingers.   And there may well be basic differences which stem from the two theological systems.

On several points concerning religion, however, a
majority of right-wingers would likely agree.   They oppose
negative treatments of religion.   They welcome books which
make "goodness exciting, and believable, and to be desired."[91]
Scholars and teachers, according to The Devil's Advocate,
should be chastised for scoffing too much and praying too little. [92]   The leaders are the ones who have lost faith: "the

majority of the total population still have faith and seldom
understand that their 'betters' do not. "[93]

NOTES

1.   Rosalie Gordon, "More Terrific 'Fiction,'" review of
     The First Team, by John Ball, America's Future,
     10 November 1972, pp. 5-7.

2.   Ralph de Toledano, "When the Big Job Is at Stake,"
     review of The Big Man, by Henry J. Taylor [and
     Convention, by Fletcher Knebel and Charles W.
     Bailey], National Review, 4 May 1964, p. 360.

3.   Robert Phelps, "What Is a Good Novel?" ibid., 28 June
     1958, pp. 40-41; and Richard McLaughlin, "Half-
     Gods of American Literature," ibid., 21 June 1968,
     pp. 19-20.

4.   Stephen Tonsor, "An Occupational Hazard," ibid., 30
     January 1960, p. 80.

5.   Rosalie Gordon, "Lighthearted and Sensible," review of
     The Ass that Went to Washington, by George Koether,
     America's Future, 31 January 1969, p. 6.

6.   Holmes Alexander, The Spirit of '76 (New Rochelle:
     Arlington House, 1966), p. 93.

7.   Holmes Alexander, Equivocal Men (Boston: Western
     Islands, 1964), p. ix.

8.   Ibid.

9.   Rosalie Gordon, "Distaff David," review of An I. O. U.
     for Emily, by Lu Gene Weldon, America's Future,
     8 December 1967, p. 6.

10. Robert Phelps, "Lyric and Precise," review of The
     Shadow of My Hand, by Holger Cahill, National Re-
     view, 21 March 1956, p. 26.

11. Robert Phelps, "In Search of Heroes," ibid., 22 Novem-
     ber 1958, p. 343.

12. John O. Beaty, Image of Life (New York: Thomas Nel-

son and Sons, 1940), p. 39.

13. Medford Evans, review of Trousered Apes, by Duncan
    Williams, American Opinion, February 1973, pp. 71-
    79; and J. M. Lalley, "Of Evil Communications,"
    Modern Age, Spring 1973, pp. 200-204.

14. Forrest Davis, "The Age of the Shrug," review of Ad-
    vise and Consent, by Allen Drury, in National Re-
    view, 29 August 1959, p. 305.

15. H. L. Hunt, Alpaca Revisited (Dallas: HLH Products,
    1967), p. 32.

16. E. Merrill Root, "An Author In Search of America,"
    American Opinion, April 1973, p. 55.

17. Ibid., p. 61.

18. Ibid., p. 49.

19. John Chamberlain, "Dean of Conservative Columnists,"
    review of Pen and Politics, by Holmes Alexander,
    in National Review, 14 July 1970, p. 743.

20. William S. Schlamm, review of Herblock's Here and
    Now, by Herbert Block, ibid., 11 January 1956, p.
    25.

21. Ibid.

22. William F. Buckley, Jr., "Al Capp at Bay," ibid., 20
    October 1970, p. 1124.

23. Ibid.

24. Root, "An Author In Search of America," p. 53.

25. Robert Phelps, review of Tall Trees Surround Us, by
    George C. Bailey, in National Review, 29 February
    1956, p. 29.

26. Stephen C. Shadegg, The Remnant (New Rochelle: Ar-
    lington House, 1968).

27. Ibid., p. 53.

28. Medford Evans, review of Captains and Kings, by Tay-
    lor Caldwell, in American Opinion, June 1972, p.
    79.

29. Ayn Rand, "Introduction to 'Calumet K,'" The Objec-
    tivist, October 1967, p. 7.

30. Taylor Caldwell, The Devil's Advocate (New York:
    MacFadden Books, 1964), p. 21.

31. Ibid., p. 31.

32. Walter Darnell Jacobs, "Home-Made Holocaust," re-
    view of Fail Safe by Eugene Burdick and Harvey
    Wheeler, in National Review, 4 December 1962, pp.
    444-45.

33. Rosalie Gordon, "Realistic, Dramatic Plot Against
    U.S.," review of Red January, by William Chamber-
    lain, in America's Future, 14 May 1965, p. 5.

34. William J. Fitzpatrick, "You Can Wait for the Movie,"
    review of The Shore Dimly Seen, by Robert Gold-
    ston and Triumph, by Philip Wylie, in National Re-
    view, 7 May 1963, p. 372.

35. Alexander, The Spirit of '76, p. 138.

36. Richard M. Weaver, "History or Special Pleading?" re-
    view of The American Historian, by Harvey Wish, in
    National Review, 14 January 1961, p. 22.

37. Hunt, Alpaca Revisited, p. 77.

38. Jeffrey Hart, "Ars Gratia Familiae," review of Making
    It, by Norman Podhoretz, in Triumph, March 1968,
    p. 28.

39. Robert O. Bowen, "The View from Beneath," review of
    Wilderness, by Robert Penn Warren [and two other
    books], in National Review, 2 December 1961, p.
    383.

40. Joan Didion, "Black and White, Read All Over," review
    of Hawaii, by James Michener, ibid., 5 December
    1959, p. 525.

41. Alexander, The Spirit of '76, p. 65.

42. Peter Crumpet, review of Sojourn of a Stranger, by
    Walter Sullivan [and The World of Suzie Wong, by
    Richard Mason], in National Review, 3 August 1957,
    p. 137.

43. John Chamberlain, "The Business Novel," review of
    The Lincoln Lords, by Cameron Hawley, ibid., 13
    February 1960, p. 111.

44. Shadegg, The Remnant, p. 166.

45. Ibid., p. 357.

46. Hunt, Alpaca Revisited, p. 70.

47. Alexander, The Spirit of '76, p. 228.

48. F. Farr, review of West of Washington, by Holmes
    Alexander, in National Review, 17 July 1962, p. 36.

49. Caldwell, The Devil's Advocate, pp. 114-15.

50. Gordon, "More Terrific 'Fiction,'" p. 5.

51. Alexander, The Spirit of '76, p. 200.

52. Ibid., p. 235.

53. Gordon, "More Terrific 'Fiction,'" p. 5.

54. Alexander, The Spirit of '76, p. 151.

55. William A. Rusher, " American Best Seller in Russia,"
    review of Meeting at a Far Meridian, by Mitchell
    Wilson, in National Review, 6 May 1961, pp. 286-
    87.

56. Shadegg, The Remnant, p. 134.

57. Vincent Miller, "Mirror, Mirror, on the Wall...," re-
    view of The Image, by Daniel J. Boorstin, in Nation-
    al Review, 13 March 1962, p. 170.

58. Weaver, "History of Special Pleading?" p. 22.

59. Jeffrey Hart, "By Ideology Possessed," review of Chil-
     dren and Others, by James Gould Cozzens, in Na-
     tional Review, 22 September 1964, p. 826.

60. Evans, review of Trousered Apes, p. 73.

61. Hunt, Alpaca Revisited, p. 107.

62. Caldwell, The Devil's Advocate, p. 33.

63. Rand, "Introduction to 'Calumet K,'" p. 9.

64. Caldwell, The Devil's Advocate, p. 23.

65. Alexander, The Spirit of '76, p. 189.

66. Caldwell, The Devil's Advocate, p. 21.

67. Rosalie Gordon, "Chillingly Prophetic Tale," review of
     When the Kissing Had to Stop, by Constantine Fitz-
     Gibbon, in America's Future, 16 February 1973, p.
     6.

68. Alexander, The Spirit of '76, p. 94.

69. Ibid., p. 204.

70. Ibid., p. 139.

71. William A. Rusher, "Modern Morality Play," review of
     A Shade of Difference, by Allen Drury, in National
     Review, 6 November 1962, p. 357.

72. Hunt, Alpaca Revisited, p. 106.

73. R. Daniel McMichael, The Journal of David Q. Little
     (New Rochelle: Arlington House, 1967), p. 104.

74. Alexander, The Spirit of '76, p. 204.

75. Shadegg, The Remnant, p. 124.

76. Rosalie Gordon, "Novel of First Magnitude," review of
     The Journal of David Q. Little, by R. Daniel Mc-
     Michael, in America's Future, 25 August 1967, pp.
     5-6.

77. Theodore Sturgeon, "A Viewpoint, a Dewpoint," review
     of The Surly Sullen Bell, by Russell Kirk [and Jour-
     ney into Tomorrow, by Robert Sheckley], in National
     Review, 12 February 1963, p. 119.

78. Rosalie Gordon, "Eye-Popping Thriller," review of The
     Elephant Valley, by Finis Farr, in America's Future,
     22 September 1967, p. 5.

79. Caldwell, The Devil's Advocate, p. 22.

80. Rand, "Introduction to 'Calumet K,'" p. 6.

81. Ibid.

82. Root, "Author in Search of America," p. 60.

83. Shadegg, The Remnant, p. 19.

84. Ibid., pp. 108-109.

85. Evans, review of Trousered Apes, p. 71.

86. Alexander, The Spirit of '76, p. 138.

87. Hunt, Alpaca Revisited, p. 49.

88. Anthony Lejeune, "To Valhalla with Twin Exhausts,"
     review of The Man with the Golden Gun, by Ian Flem-
     ing, in National Review, 7 September 1965, p. 776.

89. Finis Farr, The Elephant Valley (New Rochelle: Arling-
     ton House, 1967), p. 121.

90. Caldwell, The Devil's Advocate, p. 88.

91. Peter Crumpet, review of Sojourn of a Stranger, p. 138.

92. Caldwell, The Devil's Advocate, p. 129.

93. Evans, review of Trousered Apes, p. 75.

APPENDIX

RIGHT-WING BOOK CLUBS IN THE UNITED STATES
IN THE COLD WAR ERA*

Although little scholarly interest seems to have been
devoted to them, book clubs have in recent years grown in
size and scope to the point where one can likely find a club
which caters to his or her professional or recreational interests no matter how unpopular or esoteric they may be.
In 1972 a writer in Publishers Weekly estimated that there
were between 130 and 150 book clubs in the United States.[1]
Besides earning profits for their stockholders, the clubs offer three basic services: wide-ranging lists of books, convenient shopping, and reduced prices. Right-wing book clubs
are in a sense just one segment of a very broad, successful
part of the book marketing business. It would be surprising
if there were no such clubs since so many other interest
groups are served by one or more.

The printed, patriotic word is the major business of
right-wing groups. When one reads in Common Sense that
"90% of what you will ever know comes from reading"[2] or in
a book club's advertisement in American Opinion that "Books
are the sole medium where censorship of one sort of another
is not in control,"[3] one can understand why book publishing

---

*This is an abbreviated version of a paper read at a meet-
ing of the Canadian Association of American Studies,
Fall, 1975.

and selling hold such a central place in the activities of patriotic societies.   Books, however, are but one form of com-
munication.   Some groups concern themselves more with
pamphlets, decals, bumper stickers, records, and films than
with books.

Despite the large number of publications offered by
the hundreds of right-wing organizations, relatively few books
can, without great difficulty, claim to be works of art rather
than propaganda.   But in their efforts to influence citizens'
attitudes patriotic groups sometimes publish and frequently
endorse novels or books of poetry.   To spread the acceptable
word, they have established book clubs which feature conservative books.

So far, three book clubs that are designed for conservative readers have been established.   The Conservative
Book Club, established in 1964, is the oldest and most successful of them.   It is affiliated with Arlington House of New
Rochelle, New York.   At first its mailing address was the
same as the publisher's but it has now moved to a new one
in the same city.   Sponsors of the club included William F.
Buckley, Jr., John Dos Passos, Barry Goldwater, Will Her-
berg, Russell Kirk, and other persons who would be familiar
to readers of the National Review.   Membership has been indicated as about 30,000. [4]

Closely associated with the Conservative Book Club is
the Nostalgia Book Club.   At times it too has had a separate
address but, as of the summer of 1975, it shares one with
Conservative Book Club.   Its offerings are largely publications of Arlington House.   A few books are available from
both clubs--a biography of actor John Wayne, for example.
Occasionally advertisements in National Review give the reader a choice of securing a book from Nostalgia Club or of

ordering directly from Arlington House.   But the club does
not address itself specifically to a conservative audience as
the other three do.

Two other clubs have apparently been far less successful than the Conservative Book Club, if advertising is any in-
dication of their well-being.   In October 1972, American
Opinion (a John Birch Society publication) carried an advertisement for the Anti-Communist Book Club, with a Washington, D. C. address.   John A. Carter, membership director,
was the only person identified as an official of the club.   Apparently the project was short-lived for it did not advertise
further and mail addressed to it is returned to the sender.

A third club, Veritas, was announced twice in American Opinion: as a "pioneer" club in 1971, and as a "new"
one in 1973.   It was affiliated with the Devin-Adair Company
and had an Old Greenwich, Connecticut address.   No individuals were listed as officials.   Whereas the Conservative
Book Club is related to the Buckley "family" of organizations,
Veritas belongs in the John Birch Society grouping.   Although
it has survived for four years, the number and variety of
books offered by the club have not changed noticeably.   In
the summer of 1975, it offered the same basic choices that
it did in 1971.

The John Birch Society and its Western Islands Press
are major publishers of right-wing materials.   The society
publishes a monthly "Book News" which is free to anyone
who requests it.   But so far the organization has not attempted to develop a book club per se, with official membership, gift books, reduced rates and other features of most
book clubs.   The negative option--the provision that a member
must notify a club if he or she does not wish to receive a
book, the controversial policy which without doubt is the es-

sence of book club marketing--is not made a part of being
put on the mailing list.   Similar outlets include Libertarianism Review and Books for Libertarians (available for an an-
nual fee which is sometimes applied toward the purchase of
books), which review and sell books of interest to libertarians
but do not function as formal book clubs.

The stated purposes of the book clubs are quite similar.   At the heart of each are admitted negative motives.
The Anti-Communist Book Club indicated that identifying subversives was not enough.   It set out to "oppose the whole
left-wing spectrum. "[5]   In discussing how it would differ from
other conservative anticommunist clubs, it claimed that it
would offer books from a wide-range of publishers and not be
the sales outlet for a single house.   It also noted that its
offices were in Washington, D.C. , on the "firing line" rather
than in the ivory tower.

Veritas also makes clear that it is designed for negative purposes: to oppose "a liberal-dominated 'one world. ' "[6]
It promises to seek out books on the "other" side and to save
the reader money.   It also claims that "standards of excel-
lence maintained by the sixty-one year old Devin-Adair Company" will be used in choosing books.   Finally, it indicates
that it will be a source of books "not available in most bookstores for obvious reasons. "

The Conservative Book Club's purpose is not as negatively stated as the other two.   It acknowledges the hope that
its efforts will "add enormously to the momentum of the conservative movement and help spread conservative influence. "[7]
It promises wide-ranging subject matter and styles.   It also
describes itself as the "only major book club that provides
(as would be expected of a conservative enterprise) complete
freedom of choice and action. "   It requires no minimum

purchases but does include the negative option feature.

A survey of the materials offered by the clubs reveals
that they are not designed to distribute belle lettres.   At no
point is there an emphasis upon reading for fun, for a variety
of views.   And one is not surprised that the clubs do not offer books which are critical of conservative causes.   It is
readily apparent that the books are overwhelmingly negative
rather than positive approaches to subjects.

Anticommunism is the major subject of right-wing
book club selections.   Confessions of former Communists,
both domestic and foreign, exposure of radicals, and biogra-
phies of heroic anticommunists (such as J. Edgar Hoover)
hold a large place in right-wing club offerings.   So do economics books which glorify capitalism and oppose other economic ideologies.

Rightists tend to focus upon intellectuals as the primary villains in what they describe as the decline of the
West.   Hence many of their books focus upon "liberal establishment opinion molders. "   Two examples from the Conservative Book Club indicate the range of such books.   In June
1973, it offered Thomas Molnar's The Decline of the Intellectual as a heavy, serious study. [9]   A month earlier it had
offered This Beats Working for a Living: The Dark Secrets
of a College Professor by Professor X. [10]   The advertisement promised that the latter book would reveal such "secrets" as why professors shy away from well-written text-
books, why professors tend to be pompous, why academics
tend toward anarchy, and how to keep coeds awake in the
classroom. [11]   A few statements from the book reveal other
secrets:

> Most professors have strong feelings of inferi-
> ority to begin with, stemming from their origins.
> (p. 105)

> most academicians ... play the game of academic
> politics intuitively. (p. 136)

> The professor, in truth, finds only some
> fifteen to twenty hours of his week filled with actual
> work related to his duties. (p. 17)

Right-wing literature has much to say about youth and
the education of youth. Book clubs have offered several
studies by authors who take negative attitudes toward the public school systems of the country. And youth cultures have
provided rightists with some of their most colorful stories.
Suzanne Labin's Hippies, Drugs and Promiscuity,[12] selected
by the Conservative Book Club, paints a very gloomy picture
of what the hippie movement is all about. After two hundred
pages of material based primarily upon personal ads from
papers such as The Berkeley Barb and The Oracle, the author
reports:

> The particular part of their creed that af-
> firms that the body should be entirely free, that
> experience of every conceivable carnal pleasure, at
> every possible moment, is a great good, that every
> imaginable practice should be engaged in either with
> a partner of the opposite sex, the same sex, or no
> partner at all, is ... applied to the letter. (p. 216)

Add political subversion to sexual immorality and one
has the two themes which dominate books of literary criticism and fiction offered by right-wing book clubs. In February 1973, the Conservative Book Club selected Trousered
Apes: Sick Literature in a Sick Society by Duncan Williams.
It had been published originally in England in 1971 and was
published in the United States by Arlington House the next
year. The thesis of the book, as described by the book club,
is that "art can corrupt." The advertisement continues:

> ... the lurid themes that dominate literature and

drama today--sadism, sodomy, the drug culture,
barnyard sex--and the raw rendering of them, work
their poison into the social body.   The result is
animalism.   Trousered apes....   Two centuries of
revolt against religion, reason and order led us to
Woodstock. 13

The Conservative Book Club has selected novels as
free books for joining the club or as regular selections.
Allen Drury's Capable of Honor, Holmes Alexander's The
Spirit of '76, R. Daniel McMichael's The Journal of David
Q. Little, and Constantine FitzGibbon's When the Kissing
Had to Stop are four such books.   Veritas selected William
Craig's The Tashkent Crisis as one of its few fiction offer-
ings.

NOTES

1.   Thomas Weyl, "The Booming Book Clubs," Publishers
       Weekly, March 13, 1972, p. 32.

2.   Common Sense, May 15, 1972.

3.   Advertisement, American Opinion, May, 1973, p. 84.

4.   Ferdinand V. Solara, Key Influences in the American
       Right (Denver: Polifax Press, 1972), p. 13; and
       Holmes Alexander, Pen and Politics: Autobiography
       of a Working Writer (Morgantown: University of
       West Virginia Library, 1970).

5.   Advertisement, American Opinion, October, 1972, p.
       100.

6.   Ibid. , May, 1973, p. 84.

7.   Advertisement, National Review, June 16, 1964, p. 505.

8.   Originally published by World Publishing Co. , 1961.

9.   National Review, June 8, 1973, p. 605.

10. New Rochelle: Arlington House, 1973.

11. National Review, May 25, 1973, p. 553.

12. New Rochelle: Arlington House, 1972.

13. National Review, February 2, 1973, p. 121.

BIBLIOGRAPHY

The following listings include few secondary books and articles which are listed in general secondary studies and indexes.

Abbreviations:
AF - America's Future.
AO - American Opinion.
NR - National Review.

Asterisks:
*Paperback edition used in this study.
**Book unavailable; information based on review/s or advertisement/s.
***Book unavailable and not referred to in this study.

I. Primary Sources

A. Books

1. Novels

Alexander, Holmes. The Equivocal Men: Tales of the Establishment. Boston: Western Islands Press, 1964.

Reviewed: AF, 25 September 1964, pp. 5-6; and NR, 9 February 1965, pp. 116-17.

_____. The Spirit of '76: A Political Novel of the Near Future. New Rochelle: Arlington House, 1966.

Reviewed: AF, 17 February 1967, pp. 5-6 (with follow-up article 7 April 1967, pp. 5-7); and NR, 7 February 1967, p. 155.

_____. West of Washington. New York: Fleet Publish-
ers, 1962.

Only indirectly related to political/economic issues.
Reviewed: NR, 17 July 1962, p. 36.

*Ayer, Frederick, Jr. The Man in the Mirror. Chicago:
Henry Regnery Co. , 1965. New York: Signet Books,
1966.

Reviewed: AF, 16 July 1965, pp. 5-6.

***_____. Where No Flags Fly. Chicago: Henry Reg-
nery Co. , 1960.

Reviewed: AF, 30 September 1960.

*Ball, John. The First Team. Boston: Little, Brown and
Co. , 1971. New York: Bantam Books, 1973.

Author is not publicly identified with right-wing causes
but his book was enthusiastically received. Reviewed:
AF, 10 November 1972, pp. 5-7.

Beaty, John. Crossroads: A Novel of the Twentieth Century
South. Dallas: Wilkinson Publishing Co. , 1956.

Written in the late 1930s, published after the Supreme
Court outlawed segregation in 1954. Reviewed: NR,
16 February 1957, p. 165.

***Buckley, William F. , Jr. Saving the Queen. Garden
City: Doubleday and Co. , 1975.

Reviewed: Human Events, 7 February 1976, p. 7.

Cahill, Holger. The Shadow of My Hand. New York: Har-
court, Brace, 1956.

Author is not publicly identified with right-wing causes.
Reviewed: NR, 21 March, 1956, p. 26.

*Caldwell, Taylor. Captains and Kings. Garden City:
Doubleday and Co. , 1972. Greenwich: Fawcett Publications, 1973.

Reviewed: AO, June 1972, pp. 77ff.

*_____. The Devil's Advocate. New York: Crown Pub-
lishers, 1952. New York: MacFadden Books, 1964.

***Carney, Otis. The Paper Bullet. New York: William
Morrow Co., 1966.

Reviewed: AF, 6 May 1966, pp. 5-6.

***Chamberlain, William. Red January. New York: Paper-
back Library, 1965.

Reviewed: AF, 14 May 1965, pp. 5-6.

**Cheney, Brainerd. This Is Adam. New York: McDowell,
Obolensky, 1958.

Reviewed: NR, 6 December 1958, p. 375.

Craig, William. The Tashkent Crisis. New York: E. P.
Dutton and Co. Inc., 1971.

Chosen by Veritas Book Club, AO, July-August 1972,
pp. 46-47. Reviewed: AF, 13 August 1971, pp. 5-7.

Dixon, Thomas Jr. The Clansman: An Historical Romance
of the Ku Klux Klan. New York: Doubleday, Page
and Co., 1905. Ridgewood, N.J.: The Gregg Press,
1967.

_____. The Leopard's Spots: A Romance of the White
Man's Burden: 1865-1900. New York: Doubleday,
Page and Co., 1902. Ridgewood, N.J.: The Gregg
Press Inc., 1967.

The two Dixon novels were advertised in The Councilor as late as 1973.

Dos Passos, John. Chosen Country. Boston: Houghton
Mifflin Co., 1951.

_____. District of Columbia. Boston: Houghton Mifflin
Co., 1952.

_____. The Great Days. New York: Sagamore Press,
1968.

_____. Mid-century. Boston: Houghton Mifflin Co., 1961.

*Douglass, William Campbell. The Eagle's Feather. New
     Orleans: Free Men Speak, Inc. , 1966.

*Drury, Allen. Advise and Consent. Garden City: Double-
     day and Co. , 1959. New York: Giant Cardinal Books,
     1961.

     Reviewed: NR, 29 August 1959, pp. 305-306.

*   . Capable of Honor. Garden City: Doubleday and
     Co. , 1966. New York: Dell Books, 1968.

     Reviewed· AF, 11 November 1966, pp. 5-7 with a
     follow-up article 25 November 1966, pp. 5-7; NR, 15
     November 1966, pp. 1174-75; and The Objectivist,
     October 1966, pp. 7-12.

*   . Come Nineveh, Come Tyre. Garden City:
     Doubleday and Co. , 1973. New York: Avon Books,
     1974.

     Reviewed: AF, 23 November 1973, pp. 6-8.

          . Preserve and Protect. Garden City: Doubleday
     and Co. , 1968.

     Reviewed: AO, November 1968, pp. 70ff; AF, 25 Octo-
     ber 1968, pp. 5-6; NR, 3 December 1968, pp. 1225-
     26; and The Objectivist, December 1968, pp. 11-16
     followed by interview in January 1969, pp. 9-16.

          . The Promise of Joy. Garden City: Doubleday
     and Co. , 1975.

     Reviewed: AF, 28 March 1975, pp. 6-7 with follow-
     up article 20 June 1975, pp. 7-8.

*   . A Shade of Difference. Garden City: Doubleday
     and Co. , 1962. New York: Giant Cardinal Books,
     1963.

     Reviewed: NR, 6 November 1962, pp. 356-57.

          . The Throne of Saturn: A Novel of Space and
     Politics. Garden City: Doubleday and Co. , 1971.

     Reviewed: AF, 26 November 1971, pp. 5-7; NR, 6
     April 1971, pp. 377-78.

Farr, Finis. The Elephant Valley. New Rochelle: Arlington House, 1967.

> Offered free with subscription to AF. Reviewed: AF,
> 22 September 1967, pp. 5-6; NR, 31 October 1967,
> p. 1219.

Fitz Gibbon, Constantine. When the Kissing Had to Stop.
New York: W. W. Norton Co., 1960. New Rochelle:
Arlington House, 1973.

> Reviewed: AF, 16 February 1973, pp. 5-7.

*Fox, Victor J. [pseud.] The Pentagon Case. New York:
Freedom Press, Inc., 1958. Belmont: American
Opinion Reprint Series, 1961.

Giles, Janice Holt. Hannah Fowler. Boston: Houghton
Mifflin Co., 1956.

> Appreciated for its emphasis upon individualism. Au-
> thor not known as right-winger. Reviewed: NR, 27
> June 1956, p. 22.

Gordon, Caroline. Old Red. New York: Charles Scribner's
Sons, 1963.

> Collection of short stories endorsed by NR. Re-
> viewed: NR, 31 December 1963, p. 571; also see NR,
> 2 December 1961, p. 384.

Hunt, H. L. Alpaca Revisited. Dallas: HLH Products,
1967.

***Koether, George. The Ass That Went to Washington.
New Rochelle: Arlington House, 1968.

> Reviewed: AF, 31 January 1969, pp. 5-6.

Lumpkin, Grace. Full Circle. Boston: Western Islands
Press, 1962.

Lytle, Andrew. A Novel, a Novella and Four Stories. New
York: McDowell, Obolensky, 1958.

> Endorsed by NR, 22 November 1958, p. 348.

McMichael, R. Daniel. The Journal of David Q. Little.
    New Rochelle: Arlington House, 1967.

    Offered free with membership in Conservative Book
    Club and with subscription to America's Future. Re-
    viewed: AF, 25 August 1967, pp. 5-6; Intercollegiate
    Review, January-March 1960, pp. 112-15; and NR, 11
    July 1967, p. 753.

Mano, D. Keith. Bishop's Progress. Boston: Houghton
    Mifflin Co., 1968.

_____. The Bridge. Garden City: Doubleday and Co.,
    1973.

_____. The Death and Life of Harry Goth. New York:
    Alfred A. Knopf, 1971.

_____. Horn. Boston: Houghton Mifflin Co., 1969.

_____. The Proselytizer. New York: Alfred A. Knopf,
    1972.

    Reviewed: NR, 18 August 1972, p. 905.

_____. War Is Heaven! Garden City: Doubleday and
    Co., 1970.

    Reviewed: NR, 11 August 1970, pp. 847-48.

Prokopoff, Stephen G. A Twentieth Century Odyssey. Bos-
    ton: The Christopher Publishing House, 1961.

    Anticommunist story not referred to in this study.

Rand, Ayn. Anthem. Caldwell, Idaho: Caxton Printers,
    1961.

*_____. The Fountainhead. Indianapolis: The Bobbs-
    Merrill Co., 1943. New York: Signet Books, 1968.

    Article about reprinting, AF, 18 October 1968, pp.
    5-7.

_____. Atlas Shrugged. New York: Random House,
    1957.

*Roberts, Kenneth. Boon Island. Garden City: Doubleday
    and Co., 1955. Greenwich: Fawcett Publications,
    n. d.

    Endorsed by AO, April 1973, pp. 49ff.

Shadegg, Stephen C. The Remnant. New Rochelle: Arling-
    ton House, 1968.

    By the author of Barry Goldwater: Freedom Is His
    Flight Plan and What Happened to Goldwater. Re-
    viewed: AF, 7 June 1968, pp. 5-6.

Sullivan, Walter. Sojourn of a Stranger. New York: Henry
    Holt Co., 1957.

    Reviewed: NR, 3 August 1957, pp. 137-38.

Taylor, Henry J. The Big Man. New York: Random House,
    1964.

    Reviewed: NR, 4 May 1964, p. 360.

Webster, Merwin. Calumet "K." New York: Grosset and
    Dunlop, 1901. New York: NBI Book Service, 1967.

    Ayn Rand's Objectivist organization republished this
    book, described by Rand as her favorite novel.

Weldon, Lu Gene. An I.O.U. for Emily. New Rochelle:
    Arlington House, 1967.

    Reviewed: AF, 8 December 1967, pp. 5-6.

Woodbury, David O. Five Days to Oblivion. New York:
    The Devin-Adair Co., 1963.

    Reviewed: AF, 21 February 1964, pp. 5-7.

**_____. Mr. Farraday's Formula. New York: The
    Devin-Adair Co., 1965.

    Reviewed: AF, 8 October 1965, pp. 5-6.

**_____. You're Next on the List. Boston: Western
    Islands Press, 1968.

    Reviewed: AO, January 1969, pp. 87ff.

2. Nonfiction

Alexander, Holmes. Pen and Politics: The Autobiography
of a Working Writer. Morgantown: University of
West Virginia Library, 1970.

Reviewed: AO, February 1970, pp. 79ff. ; and NR,
14 July 1970, pp. 742-43.

Beaty, John O. Image of Life. New York: Thomas Nelson
and Sons, 1940.

A book of literary criticism endorsed by right-wing
journals. By author of Crossroads.

_____. The Iron Curtain Over America. Dallas: Wilkin-
son Publishing Co. , 1951.

Caldwell, Taylor. Dialogues with the Devil. Garden City:
Doubleday and Co. , Inc. , 1967.

Reviewed: AO, June 1967, pp. 41ff. Also available
in Fawcett Crest paperback edition.

_____. On Growing Up Tough. New York: The Devin-
Adair Co. , 1971. Greenwich: Fawcett Publications,
1972.

Collection of essays from American Opinion. Reviewed: AO, June 1971, pp. 73-77.

Dos Passos, John. The Fourteenth Chronicle: Letters and
Diaries of John Dos Passos. Boston: Gambit, 1973.

Reviewed: The Alternative, October 1974, p. 21.

_____. Occasions and Protests. Chicago: Henry Reg-
nery Co. , 1964.

Probably the best received of Dos Passos' books
among right-wing critics. Reviewed: AF, 23 April
1964, pp. 5-6; Intercollegiate Review, January 1965,
pp. 80-85; Modern Age, Summer 1965, pp. 296-301;
and University Bookman, Autumn 1965, pp. 18-23.

_____. The Theme Is Freedom. New York: Dodd,
Mead and Co. , 1956.

Reviewed: NR, 23 May 1956, pp. 19-20.

_____. World in a Glass: A View of Our Century from the Novels of John Dos Passos. Edited by Kenneth S. Lynn. Boston: Houghton, Mifflin Co. , 1966.

Reviewed: NR, 24 January 1967, pp. 93ff.

Farr, Finis. Margaret Mitchell. New York: Morrow, 1965.

Biography of a writer endorsed by right-wingers. By the author of The Elephant Valley. See also AO, May 1968, front cover and statement on back cover, about Mitchell.

_____. O'Hara: A Biography. Boston: Little, Brown and Co. , 1973.

Fuller, Edmund. Man in Modern Fiction. New York: Random House, 1958.

Recommended in White Book of the John Birch Society, 1961, "Initial List of Approved Books"; Recommended by Human Events, 16 June 1958, p. 3.

Gardiner, Harold C. Editor. American Classics Reconsidered: A Christian Appraisal. New York: Charles Scribner's Sons, 1958.

Reviewed: NR, 21 June 1958, pp. 19-20.

Hart, Jeffrey. The American Dissent: A Decade of Modern Conservative Thought. Garden City: Doubleday and Co. , Inc. , 1966.

Passing references to fiction.

Hook, Sidney. The Fail-Safe Fallacy. New York: Stein and Day, 1963. [Booklet].

Reviewed: NR, 19 November 1963, pp. 444-45.

Kenner, Hugh. A Homemade World: The American Modernist Writers. New York: Alfred A. Knopf, 1973.

Reviewed: The Alternative, September 1975, pp. 23-

24; and NR, 23 May 1975, pp. 568-69.

Kirk, Russell. Enemies of Permanent Things: Observations of Abnormality in Literature. New Rochelle: Arlington House, 1969.

Reviewed: AO, May 1969, pp. 79ff.

Lytle, Andrew. The Hero with the Private Parts. Baton Rouge: Louisiana State University Press, 1966.

Phelps, Robert. Heroes and Orators. New York: McDowell, Obolensky, 1958.

Listed as one of the outstanding books of 1958, NR, 22 November 1958, p. 348.

Post, Clinton Thomas. The Conservative Crime: A View of the Political and Social Scene of Our Time. New York: Exposition Press, 1968.

A "conservative" writer's complaints about discrimination.

Rand, Ayn. The Romantic Manifesto: A Philosophy of Literature. New York: New American Library, Signet Book, 1971. Originally published by World Publishing Co., 1969.

Root, E. Merrill. America's Steadfast Dream. Boston: Western Islands Press, 1971. Paperback edition, 1974.

Collection of essays from American Opinion by longtime professor of English at Earlham College. Introduction by Taylor Caldwell.

Sedlmayr, Hans. Art in Crisis: The Lost Center. Chicago: Henry Regnery Co., 1958.

Recommended in Human Events, 16 June 1958, p. 3.

Stearn, Jess. The Search for a Soul: Taylor Caldwell's Psychic Lives. Garden City: Doubleday and Co., 1972. Greenwich: Fawcett Publications, 1974.

Tuccille, Jerome. It Usually Begins with Ayn Rand. New

York: Stein and Day, 1971.

Helpful in understanding relationship of libertarianism to right-wing ideology.

Williams, Duncan. Trousered Apes: Sick Literature in a Sick Society. London: Churchill Press, Ltd. , 1971. New Rochelle: Arlington House, 1973.

Reviewed: AO, February 1973, pp. 71ff; and Modern Age, September 1973, pp. 200-204.

3. Others

Bailey, George C. Tall Trees Surround Us. Caldwell, Idaho: Caxton Printers, 1955.

Nonfiction account of homesteading on a former Indian reservation. Reviewed: NR, 29 February 1956, pp. 28-29.

Capp, Al. The Hardhat's Bedtime Story Book. New York: Harper and Row, 1971.

Reviewed: AF, 19 November 1971, pp. 5-7; and AO, October 1971, pp. 91-92.

Chapman, M. Winslow (Mrs.). Key Hole. Memphis: Windermere Press, 1967.

Poetry. Reviewed: AO, May 1967, pp. 107-108.

Eff, Johannes. Effigies: Poems from the National Review. Montgomery, Calif. : F/B Books, 1970.

Reviewed: NR, 23 February 1971, p. 204.

Grimes, Martin. Turnip Greens and Sergeant Stripes. New Rochelle: Arlington House, 1972.

"Humorous" tall tales by a southern retired Army master sergeant. Reviewed: NR, 29 September 1972, p. 1071.

Hooper, Lucille. The Patent Leather Thumping Shoes. Caldwell, Idaho: Caxton Printers, 1956.

Recommended by NR as worth reading, 1956.

Meyer, Frank S.   Editor.   Breathes There the Man: Heroic
Ballads and Poems of the English-Speaking Peoples.
LaSalle, Ill.: Open Court Publishing Co. , 1974.

Reviewed: AO, June 1974, pp. 92-93.

Morse, Douglas.   The Ballad of John Birch: After the Prose
of Robert Welch.   Brookfield, Mass.: The Country
Press, 1964.

Foreword by E. Merrill Root.

Ranuzzi, F. X.   The Death of Joe McCarthy.   Los Angeles:
Poor Richard's Book Shop, n. d.

Poems.

Tyrmand, Leopold.   The Rosa Luxemburg Contraceptive Cooperative: A Primer in Communist Civilization.   New
York: The Macmillan Co. , 1972.

Reviewed: The Alternative, February 1973; AF, 16
June 1972, pp. 5-7; AO, December 1972, pp. 87ff. ;
and NR, 26 May 1972, p. 590.

von Dreele, W. H.   If Liberals Had Feathers.   New York:
Devin-Adair Co. , 1968.

Reviewed: AO, February 1968, pp. 101-102.

_____ .   There's Something About a Liberal.   New Rochelle: Arlington House, 1970.

Introductory note by Barry Goldwater.   Reviewed:
AO, April 1971, pp. 89ff. ; and NR, 23 February
1971, p. 204.

B.   Periodicals

The Alternative.   From the Mountain.

America's Future.   Human Events.

American Opinion.   Intercollegiate Review.

Modern Age.   Quillon.

National Review.   Triumph.

The Objectivist.   University Bookman.

C.   Articles

Beum, Robert.   "The Natural Law of Poetry. "   Triumph,
    November 1968, pp. 34-37.

Buckley, F. Reid.   "Liberalism and Literature. "   Triumph,
    February 1968, pp. 26-27.

Evans, Medford.   "Taylor Caldwell. "   American Opinion,
    October 1971, pp. 31-42.

Fish, Lazy Jo.   "Fiction and Conservatives. "   The Alterna-
    tive, April 1971, pp. 8-9.

Grumbach, Doris.   "The State of the Novel in the Seventies. "
    The Alternative, December 1975, pp. 10-11.

Rand, Ayn.   "Basic Principles of Literature. "   The Objec-
    tivist, July 1968, pp. 1-8.

Robbins, John W.   "Conservatism versus Objectivism. "   In-
    tercollegiate Review, Winter 1969-70, pp. 41-49.

Root, E. Merrill.   "Mark Twain. "   American Opinion, Janu-
    ary 1968, p. 113.

U. S. Congress.   Senate.   Senator J. Strom Thurmond speak-
    ing on "The Suppression of Books. "   90th Cong. , 1st
    sess. , 21 February 1967, vol. 133, pp. 4120-4124.

Wittmer, Felix.   "The Atrophy of Arts and Letters in Our
    General-History Textbooks. "   University Bookman,
    Spring 1962, pp. 61ff.

II.   Secondary Sources

Blotner, Joseph.   The Modern American Political Novel.
    Austin: University of Texas Press, 1966.

Dickinson, A. T. Jr.   American Historical Fiction.   3rd ed.
    Metuchen, N.J.:   Scarecrow Press, Inc., 1971.

Egger, Rowland.   "The Administrative Novel."   American
    Political Science Review 53 (June 1959): 448-55.

Hugo, Grant.   "The Political Influence of the Thriller."
    Contemporary Review, December 1972, pp. 284-89.

Morrison, Louise Douglas.   "The Modern Presidency in
    American Fiction."   PhD. dissertation.   American
    Studies.   Case Western Reserve University, 1972.

Solara, Ferdinand V.   Key Influences in the American Right.
    Denver: Polifax Press, 1972.

Spegele, Roger D.   "Fiction and Political Theory."   Social
    Research 38 (Spring 1971): 108-38.

Wilcox, Laird M.   Guide to the American Right.   Kansas
    City, Mo.:   U.S. Directory Service, 1970.

INDEX